Why Can't We Say What We Mean?

By Jed A. Reay

Presented by
www.jedthecommunicator.com

Copyright © 2008. Jed A. Reay. All rights reserved.

www.jedthecommunicator.com

NOTICE

ALL RIGHTS RESERVED. This book contains material protected under International and Federal Copyright Laws and Treaties. Any unauthorized reprint or use of this material is prohibited.

No part of this book may be reproduced or transmitted in any form or by any means, electronic or mechanical, including photocopying, recording, or by any information storage and retrieval system without express written permission from the author and publisher.

Copyright © 2008. Jed A. Reay. All rights reserved.

Why Can't We Say What We Mean?

DISCLAIMER

The information presented in this book represents the sole view of the authors and publishers and is intended for informational purposes only as of the date of publication. All content represents the sole opinions of the authors and publishers without bias on the part of the authors.

The information contained in this book is strictly for educational purposes. No guarantees are made that the reader will achieve results similar to the ideas and techniques discussed in this book.

Examples cited in this book are not to be interpreted as a personal recommendation, nor are they to be interpreted as representative results.

The reader takes full responsibility for his or her actions and all consequences associated with those actions when applying or attempting to apply ideas stated in this book.

All references are for informational purposes only and the authors and publishers are released from and the reader is

Copyright © 2008. Jed A. Reay. All rights reserved.

www.jedthecommunicator.com

responsible for any subjective decision made as to their content and / or use.

For questions or comments concerning this book please visit www.jedthecommunicator.com

Copyright © 2008. Jed A. Reay. All rights reserved.

Why Can't We Say What We Mean?

TABLE OF CONTENTS

ACKNOWLEDGMENTS	9
INTRODUCTION	14
CHAPTER 1: INTERVIEW WITH LARRY BENET	20
CHAPTER 2: INTERVIEW WITH RYAN CELESTAIN	36
CHAPTER 3: INTERVIEW WITH SETH DALEY	53
CHAPTER 4: INTERVIEW WITH KATRINA FERGUSON	66
CHAPTER 5: INTERVIEW WITH KANDEE G	86
CHAPTER 6: INTERVIEW WITH DR. FRAN HARRIS	99
CHAPTER 7: INTERVIEW WITH DR. STAN HARRIS	122
CHAPTER 8: INTERVIEW WITH ARTEMIS LIMPERT	154
CHAPTER 9: INTERVIEW WITH TIM MCKEE	196
CHAPTER 10: INTERVIEW WITH LYNN PIERCE	215
CHAPTER 11: INTERVIEW WITH STEPHEN PIERCE	236

Copyright © 2008. Jed A. Reay. All rights reserved.

www.jedthecommunicator.com

CHAPTER 12:
 INTERVIEW WITH STEVEN SADLEIR 255

CHAPTER 13:
 INTERVIEW WITH JOEL THERIEN 273

CONCLUSION 304

Copyright © 2008. Jed A. Reay. All rights reserved.

Why Can't We Say What We Mean?

MEET JED REAY

Mr. Jed A. Reay

Jed Reay began his entrepreneurial adventures at the age of 12. Thirty-nine years later he is still writing life's script. He is a graduate of the University of Oregon with a Master's Degree in Business Communication. In 1986, Jed was selected to the *Who's Who Among Students in Universities and Colleges*, in 1991 to the *Emerging Leaders in America*, and in 1992 to the *Among Young American Professionals*.

While still in college, Jed and another student, partner R. Scott Martin, started FMR Business Consulting. This company was a pilot project for their business communication class, but also grew to be a very successful consulting firm that analyzed corporate communication to better assist that management on how to improve their bottom lines by way of improving the internal corporate culture.

Jed has started several other businesses in the medical field, which grew to produce over $2.5 million in annual sales. Jed has since moved on to

Copyright © 2008. Jed A. Reay. All rights reserved.

other projects, which now help others build off of his 30 years of experience.

Currently, Jed is a business development consultant. He has helped to form an organization of like-mined entrepreneurs that assists those seeking to venture out on their own and make those same life-changing decisions. Jed has helped thousands of people all over the world realize their dreams. He teaches and trains individuals and groups to achieve their full potential in the business world.

"This vision has not come to me lightly. I often reflect on a short verse I found some years ago by an unknown author. I live this with all my heart and soul."

> "Excellence can be attained if you care more than others think is wise, risk more than others think is safe, dream more than others think is practical, and expect more than others think is possible."

It is with all my passion and desire that as you read this, you are truly inspired to stretch your imagination, expect more from yourself, and achieve your true destiny.

Jed A. Reay
"The Communicator"

Copyright © 2008. Jed A. Reay. All rights reserved.

Why Can't We Say What We Mean?

ACKNOWLEDGMENTS

This book is dedicated to all those souls with the passion and desire to live their dreams, live their visions, and as my close friend and mentor says, live "a freedom-filled life." Tim, you inspire me. Thank you.

This book is also dedicated to my wife, Gina, for her unwavering spirit and devotion, and her ability to see past my weaknesses and show me my strengths.

To my daughter and son, Kayla and Joshua, with your young minds and child-like nature, you have helped me imagine and truly dream again.

Alicia Pierce, this project would not have taken on its own life if not for you. I humbly thank you from the bottom of my heart. I am truly blessed to know you and call you a friend. This is all possible because of you.

And a very special thank you goes to Cynthia Bull, my chief editor and all-around rally squad when it comes to putting this book together. I can say without hesitation that I cannot live without her insight and guidance. Cynthia, our future looks very bright. I thank you from the bottom of my heart. You are a Godsend.

To the contributors who have helped to make this book what it is, and me what I am today, I stand in awe of what you have done for me, and what our

Copyright © 2008. Jed A. Reay. All rights reserved.

relationships can do for many who will read this and other works.

Larry Benet, "The Connector," thank you, sir, for showing me how simple, truly simple it is to make a connection, more importantly a connection of value to the person you are connecting with. You have been an inspiration to me, and I thank you from the bottom of my heart.

Ryan Celestain, my friend and vocal personality of the radio waves, without your uplifting spirit, communication and the sharing of ideas would be mundane and a bit of a bore. You have helped me to focus on my inspiration and lead me to know my outcomes.

Seth Daley, for your willingness to play the role of director and not allow me to get off track and lose focus, you have also proven to me that young minds can teach old dogs new tricks. I am in your debt and I can say, "I truly love you, brother."

Katrina Ferguson, it is that total woman that makes you very special. I thank you so very much for you guidance and assistance with this project. Your honesty, directness, and boldness have given me more perspective on rewriting my purpose and discovering my true potential.

Kandee G, all I can say is, "WOW!" You bring a powerful spirit and energy to my soul. Prior to this project, I will have to admit I really did not have a lot of powerful women in my life. I can now say I have several, and you are one of them. Your energy,

Why Can't We Say What We Mean?

focus, and dedication inspired me to continue on a road less traveled. I thank you from the bottom of my heart.

Dr. Fran Harris, you have given me such HOPE! You amazed me from the moment we began speaking, which left me with a very special sense of energy. Your unique energy and special gifts of giving have renewed my belief in the human potential. This book would not be complete without you. I thank you deeply and look forward to exploring this relationship further.

"Dr. Breakthrough," Dr. Stan Harris, every project needs energy. No, I mean ENERGY! Your successes in the direct marketing industry give you a unique perspective on the issue facing entrepreneurs in the marketplace. You are a testament to discipline and focus. Without your spirit-filled energy, we all would be lost and wondering without purpose.

Artemis Limpert, a very special friend, who has seen me through some pretty rough times, I can't begin to thank you for all that you have done. Therefore, I will just prove to the world that you are the master. You have encouraged me to own my own greatness through tough love, and often painful directness. Without your guidance, I would not be here today.

Tim McKee, my friend and mentor, I applaud you for helping me become the maven I am. From our early beginnings, I had no idea what you had in store for me when you saw those first videos way back when. You helped me find my creative self. Without that, none of this was possible.

Lynn Pierce, the kindred spirit with whom I have found much common ground, I am blessed to have met you. The insight you brought to this project is both inspiring and thought provoking. I found your success-minded attitudes and beliefs to be powerful and learnable. Our readers will benefit greatly from your input.

Stephen Pierce and your rock Alicia, without whom this project would not have had a glimmer of hope, it is to you both that I give many thanks. Your direction and encouragement have been so freely given. I thank you with a spirit-filled heart. You give so much of yourselves to improve the lives of those around you. Stephen, I am truly indebted to you. Thank you.

Steven Sadleir, my spiritualist, you have saved my life, or should I say, awakened my spirit, which I allowed to fall asleep. There are not enough words to say how important you are to my spirit and the spirit of the human race. I love you, brother, and I will always be striving to be with you in spirit.

Joel Therien, you brought this all back into perspective for me. When I started this project I had blinders on about the nature of effective communication, when it came to the Internet and modern modes of communication. My friend, you helped me to see again. You helped me see that it is really our own responsibility to use the technology to help, rather than to harm. I can now say that

Why Can't We Say What We Mean?

because of who you are, we have begun a lifelong journey together. I look forward to collaborating on many more projects together.

To those of you unnamed supporters, I thank you from the bottom of my heart.

To those real, true heroes in my book, those doubters, those disbelievers, and that includes you, my little monkey who continues to say you will fail, thanks! Go take a hike!

Copyright © 2008. Jed A. Reay. All rights reserved.

www.jedthecommunicator.com

INTRODUCTION

Over the last 27 years of my business career, which is much longer than that, but I don't count the paper route and lawn mowing jobs as a career, I have come to realize that on some occasions human communication has not evolved much past the cave man, while at other times over-communication appears to have transcended far into the future. It is this dichotomy which has prompted me to write this book.

I am reminded of a brief conversation I had one day with my 18-year-old daughter. We were talking about my dirty hands. She made the comment that my keyboard is dirtier than the toilet bowl. I responded with, "That's great. I don't have to worry. I don't play the piano."

She burst out laughing, "You bonehead, I'm talking about your computer keyboard!"

"Oops! Oh, then mine are filthy" I responded.

This is a prime example of the potential for misunderstanding when words are spoken to communicate a message. It is quite another to write that message and hope to express and deliver yourself with the proper emotion and tone of what you wish to say.

History, personal experiences, culture, and environment are among the many variables that play a part in the way we understand something

Copyright © 2008. Jed A. Reay. All rights reserved.

Why Can't We Say What We Mean?

spoken or written. Poor communication between two people, or groups of people, is not a new or novel issue. What is new and becoming more complex is the way we communicate in the modern age of computers, with emails, text messages, audio, video, and the entire process of the communication age.

Today, we communicate and interact in a far larger environment that ever before. Within minutes of sending an email, you can communicate with one or thousands of individuals all over the world within seconds of pushing the Send button.

The opportunity is awesome, great, fantastic, but it also carries with it the responsibilities of listening, understanding, and the true desire to bridge the potential gaps technology presents.

This problem can be complicated even further when you add an international marketplace to the mix. The international landscape is complicated further because of the growth of Internet marketing and the small business industry, otherwise known as the home-based business industry.

The notion of international business is not a new idea. International trade and international business have been with us since the days of Columbus. Today, what makes conducting business internationally so challenging is the explosive nature due to the computer and the Internet.

You can literally put up a website, set up a Google account, and begin getting traffic in a few minutes.

Copyright © 2008. Jed A. Reay. All rights reserved.

This is where the communication issues and challenges are so critical. This is the reason I wanted to write about the varying degrees of human communication and the effects of such on your business in the ever-exploding world of the Internet.

I began my communication career as a counselor and therapist in 1981. I then went back to school and received my Master's Degree from the University of Oregon in communications, with a subspecialty in business communications. While that was a good education, it just prepared me for mass confusion in the dynamically, every-changing world of business.

Jump forward 20 plus years. We have mom and pop businesses opening up in the "home- based business" arena every day. Because of the nature of the computer, the Internet, and the ability to touch an unlimited audience, I see a need to understand the nature of communication in more detail.

This book will be both provocative and informative, and I truly encourage dialogue when the subject is featured. I have amassed an eclectic group of individuals from the business world to provide their own thoughts and opinions on the subject of communication in the current business climate.

The computer age… the age of right now, right now, RIGHT NOW!

In the past, we have seen that communication can be used to control and manipulate massive groups to believe and behave in a very negative way. While I

Copyright © 2008. Jed A. Reay. All rights reserved.

Why Can't We Say What We Mean?

will not give this discussion any more energy, I say that I will use negative, or don't-wants, as a contrast.

Contrast is critical for understating what communication is and what it is not. What communication is, is healthy and productive. You should learn to communicate from positions of serving and aiding others.

Do you think that being a good communicator is innate, or is it learned? Just think about the people you know that have the skills to be able to talk and connect with anyone, and then answer that question.

As a business owner, I know that I need a continuous stream of customers. In order for that to happen, I must have meaningful conversations with several people per day. I know that in order for my business to be successful, I must have these meaningful conversations with people from all walks of life, from varied backgrounds and viewpoints.

One thing that is common among all is the fact that all of them want to improve the quality of their lives. Whether it is more money, more time, freedom from a job, more family time, or just plain change, you must have meaningful conversations with others in order to know what they really want.
Meaningful conversations are not difficult to have and don't require a lot of knowledge. Just practice asking questions and listening. When you listen, you will learn a lot more than if you're talking all of the time. What a novel idea!

Copyright © 2008. Jed A. Reay. All rights reserved.

Seriously, in order to communicate with someone and move them from one position to another, you must have the ability to have that meaningful conversation.

One of the first keys to having a meaningful conversation and connecting with someone is to first and foremost be genuinely interested in what they want. If you truly desire to connect with someone and you wish to move them in a specific direction, that is, to join you, to buy from you, or to become a link to others for you, then you must first find out what you can do for them.

Far too many times the individual who is trying to move person A from here to there is only concerned with him or herself, and not the connection and not what person A really wants. This is a critical distinction that must be made in order to be successful in any business environment. The other person must trust you. If someone doesn't trust you, then they will not be moved to take action.

Secondly, if you don't put them first and you second, you may never find out that they have a sphere of influence of the hundreds of like-minded people that will also join or buy from you, or be moved from point A to point B.

Finally, if you don't recognize these issues and make adjustments as you go along, you will continue to receive very poor results in your relationships where communication is the issue.

Copyright © 2008. Jed A. Reay. All rights reserved.

Why Can't We Say What We Mean?

Always remember that this is a two-way street, but you must give first.

www.jedthecommunicator.com

CHAPTER 1: INTERVIEW WITH LARRY BENET

Mr. Larry Benet

Larry Benet is known as "The Connector" and "The Connector to Billionaires & Millionaires," providing resources that can take your business to the next level. He is considered one of the country's most outside-the-box business strategists, a master relationship builder, and has been referred to as *"America's Connection Expert."* As past Chairman of the Tsunami Disaster Relief Project, he brought top business leaders together to raise money for the victims of the tsunami.

Larry is **President of the Speakers and Authors Networking Group**, made up of some of the world's most prominent and influential speakers and authors. He has shared platforms with or interviewed people like Mark Victor Hansen, Ken Blanchard, Ken Kragen, Les Brown, Harvey MacKay, marketing geniuses Jay Abraham, Dan Kennedy, Joe Sugarman, and many other dynamic personalities.

Copyright © 2008. Jed A. Reay. All rights reserved.

Why Can't We Say What We Mean?

Larry is the founder and Chief Idea Officer of **Outside The Box Consulting, LLC**, a successful and innovative sales, marketing and promotions consulting firm.

For more information on how to become "connected," visit Larry at www.larrybenet.com and sign up for "The Connector's Newsletter."

INTERVIEW

JED: Hey, this is Jed Reay, "The Communicator." I'd like to welcome to the call Larry Benet, "The Connector," and thank him for his assistance on this book.

Some of you may know Larry and some of you may not, but by the time we're done with this conversation, you'll know very well who this man is.

Larry, I'd like to welcome you to the call and thank you very much for taking time out of your real busy schedule to stop by and chat with us.

LARRY: No problem, I appreciate the opportunity.

JED: Larry, this book is addressing issues around communication. First of all, let me just start off with just a quick synopsis of who you are and what services you're providing to the world.

LARRY: Sure. You talk about "The Communicator." I think today a lot of business is driven by relationships, and yet, I think some people are just naturally gifted. If you study most industries, normally the top people are not only thoughtful leaders, but they're also very well connected, very well plugged into their communities, depending on what kind of business. It could be very statewide or even nationally recognized, in terms of resources and strategic relationships.

One of the things I really teach is communication strategies, strategies that connect with anyone, anytime, anywhere. More importantly, how do you create a meaningful relationship, especially with a high-profile, busy, influential leader in someone's industry?

That's pretty much what we're really good at. I've had the good fortune of connecting with the likes of Larry King and one of the wealthiest people in the world.

Why Can't We Say What We Mean?

What I found is that in any industry, it's all pretty much the same. If you can fundamentally help other people and you can pretty much offer value, to me, that's the "mission critical" ingredient to connect and build relationships with anyone.

I think a lot of people don't believe that they can add value. What I try to teach is how they can create value with anyone that they ultimately come in contact with, and try to be more targeted and more strategic. Since I believe not all relationships are created equal, not all networks are created equal.

Some people in every industry just kind of have a lot more influence and a lot more reach. If you can ultimately cultivate a network of relationships with those kinds of people, it's going to be a lot easier to get referrals. It'll be a lot easier to grow your business and really get the word out about your business.

JED: You almost answered my very first question. Thank you very much. What is the biggest barrier that people need to break through in order to communicate more effectively? That was the first question. In a way, you've almost answered part of it.

LARRY: I'd say it's probably two-fold. One is the belief in themselves to communicate effectively, clearly, and really have that belief, like I said, to deliver value. I also think the other component is really knowing what they bring to the table.

For example, one of the gentlemen that I was fortunate to connect with, probably a year and one-half ago, used to be one of the wealthiest people in the United States. At one time, he was the 25th wealthiest person in America. His name is Bill Bartmann.

When I first connected with him, I think I asked him a couple of questions. We were at a charity function. Again, I didn't know him, but we had a mutual connection, so that did help. A gentleman named Charlie "Tremendous" Jones introduced us.

I remember telling Bill that his life read like a Hollywood movie, because he went from being homeless to billionaire, having

Why Can't We Say What We Mean?

minimum wage earnings to in excess of $100 million in a year.

The two questions I asked him were, "What do you do today, what are you most excited about?" and "What is the most important project you are currently working on?"

He shared two things. One, he wanted to put 70,000 kids in Texas Stadium to talk to them about the importance of self-esteem and self confidence. The other thing that he shared with me is he wanted to get his message in front of 10 million people over the next five to ten years.

Again, I didn't know him, but I took that information, and I said, "Okay, what can I do? Who do I know? How can I add value to this individual who I just met?"

As a result, I did a of couple things. I reached out to a friend of mine named Alex Mandossian and, literally, asked him the very same thing. I met Bill around the same time I had reconnected with Alex, so I asked Alex what was the most important project that he was working on, and he said something called "Virtual Seminar Week."

I said, "Okay, what are you looking for?"

He said he was looking for a whale.

And I said, "Well, that's interesting. The only whale I know is across the street at Sea World, except I don't have a strong relationship with him. What do you mean by that?"

He said he was looking for a whale of a speaker for his Virtual Seminar Week.

I said, "Well, I just met some guy named Bill Bartmann, who used to be National Entrepreneur of the Year and is a phenomenal business person that appeals to a lot of entrepreneurs. Will there be any value in me connecting you with him?"

Alex said, "As a matter of fact, that'll be awesome."
From there, I connected the two of them and that worked out real well.

Another individual, who at the time I didn't know, I connected with a gentleman named David Fry. I literally happened to recognize

Why Can't We Say What We Mean?

David at a seminar, because I was actually on his newsletter list at the time.

Again, it was the same thing. After a conversation I asked David what he was working on and what his most important project was. At the time he was working on *Millionaire Blueprints Magazine*.

He said, "Well, I'm looking for somebody, a very high-profile name that would appeal to entrepreneurs that I might be able to give away a DVD or a CD to any new subscriber of the magazine."

And I said, "Well, that's interesting. I just met some guy named Bill Bartmann. Maybe I can connect you with him." And that's exactly what happened.

It was good for David, and he ended up being able to give a DVD away. And like I said with Alex Mandossian, Bill ended up becoming one of the keynote speakers for his Virtual Seminar Week.

These were all people that, at the time, I didn't know or I didn't know that well. It just goes to show you, when you can tap in. And here's one of the underlying keys in communicating and building those relationships, is really finding out what's important to someone. It's really not all that hard to do.

I believe if you have rapport, you believe and have that confidence in yourself that you can add value, those kinds of things really go well and play to your advantage.

JED: It's really interesting to hear you say that, because the underlying theme of everything that you just said so far has always been about someone else first. You're providing value to them. Then that value's being provided back to you.

That leads me into the third question, because you already answered the second one. We won't even go into that.

There are some people that are natural communicators, others are not. What keys can you give our audience, the average person, to open the doors of communication? What kind of steps or keys or plan of action would you suggest to them?

Why Can't We Say What We Mean?

LARRY: In terms of just ability to communicate with others?

JED: Yes, just to improve that relationship, that communication. Obviously, that's the whole point of communicating at a healthy level, to nurture relationships and to improve the quality of that relationship.

LARRY: Are we talking in terms of communicating face-to-face, or are we talking over the phone?

JED: No, I think any form of communication. Obviously, the whole point of why we did this was because the form of communication that a lot of us are using is email, the faceless websites to communicate our message. Sometimes those communications are misconstrued, are not well delivered.

As someone reading this book, or if they listen to the audios or watch the video interviews, they see you and me and all of the participants communicating. But it doesn't have to be a one-on-one, face-to-face, no.

LARRY: First of all, one of the things I like to try to do is to figure out how to gain rapport with somebody. When I have the opportunity, one of the things I like to do is I like to do my research. I like to do my homework in advance.

For example, I know that you're friends with Artemis Limpert. I may bring that up as a way of gaining rapport.

If I were to meet you in person, I might stand very similar to you. I'm from New York. Where are you from, Jed?

JED: Born and raised in Oregon.

LARRY: Oregon, okay. Maybe someone in Oregon talks a little bit slower than maybe someone in New York, so I might slow down my speech patterns to match and mirror the individual that I'm trying to connect with.

These are some simple little techniques and ideas that I like to use that really allow for improved levels of communication.

The other thing, I think, because you were talking about it earlier, in terms of building the meaningful relationships and communicating, is follow-up.

Why Can't We Say What We Mean?

If you and I have a conversation and we meet in person and we talk about, "Hey, I'm willing to help you with this interview," but I don't follow through, I believe I don't hurt you. But I believe no matter how small the commitment level is, I think those who are excellent communicators are also very good at pretty much keeping commitments.

Those very simple little things, I think, really go a long way. That's one of the reasons why I picked up the phone, even though I knew I was extremely busy, so I can get back to you.

JED: Right. I really appreciate that. I know that you're in a hurry. We'll get one more question in here and we'll let you go.

The question is two-fold. Do you have services and products that you can share with our audience so that they may have some resources that they can come in contact with to help them better understand who you are, and what it is that you're trying to accomplish?

LARRY: We have different CDs and programs. I believe our strength is in

Copyright © 2008. Jed A. Reay. All rights reserved.

www.jedthecommunicator.com

connecting meaningful relationships. I believe your ability to connect with another human being, whether it's in person, over the phone or via email, is absolutely critical.

What we happen to be very good at is teaching people how to do that quickly, and how to do that in an impactful way so you can build a deep, meaningful relationship.

What I would recommend is to have people go to www.larrybenet.com That would probably be the easiest way for people to learn a little bit more on how we might be able to help.

I probably have just a couple more minutes. If you want to, I can answer another quick question or two.

JED: Thank you very much. Hopefully, this last question won't take an hour.

As a teacher, trainer, mentor, human change agent, you have a lot of powerful influence over those of us out in the world, those of us you communicate with, those of us that you connect with. You have a powerful influence, and in order to maintain that vision, that direction, that thirst, that hunger, it takes a lot

Why Can't We Say What We Mean?

of energy. The last time I looked, you didn't have a big "S" on your chest.

What is it that you do to keep yourself healthy, to keep yourself jazzed, to keep yourself coming back, and to keep doing what you do?

LARRY: I'll tell you. To me, there are a couple of things. I think your environment is really critical. Whatever your environment is, hopefully, it's a positive one that makes you feel good and gives the positive vibes.

Obviously, I think nutrition is critical. Then the thing that I believe which is really important is your ability to mastermind and connect with the right type of people.

What's interesting is just the other day I was feeling down for whatever reason, and one of the guys that I communicate with on a regular basis, who's a big mover and shaker in his own regard, said to me, "You know, I just want to congratulate you for doing as much as you do for the world, and how you help so many people and how you try to give back."

Just that brief little conversation that we had was a really big boost for me. That's why it's so important to surround yourself with other like-minded people.

If you're trying to improve your communication skills, find other people that are excellent communicators. If you're trying to improve your network or your relationships, connect and build a group of people that are superior at building relationships.

Charlie "Tremendous" Jones once said, "The person you become is going to be the books you read, the tapes you listen to, and the people you surround yourself with."

That couldn't be more true, at least for me.

JED: Oh, thank you. I agree so much with you, with regard to that.

Larry, I cannot tell you how much I appreciate the time that you've given me and our audience. I truly, truly do appreciate that, and I can't begin to thank you enough.

Why Can't We Say What We Mean?

                    With that, I'll let Larry go. He's on his way to another meeting, and a very, very busy man. We appreciate the time that you've given us.

LARRY: Thank you. Have a wonderful day. I look forward to connecting with you in person.

CHAPTER 2:
INTERVIEW WITH
RYAN CELESTAIN

Mr. Ryan Celestain

Ryan Celestain is an energetic, innovative, and **Rising Internet Star** who has mastered the art of self-branding. Ryan was able to reach over 170,000 people in 30 days promoting his primary business without spending a dime on advertising.

He received calls and emails from top Internet marketers, personal development gurus, professional athletes, authors, and even celebrity figures, all of whom went to him. He was asked to partner with noted professional fitness trainer, mentor and radio host of "Dare to Dream," Greg Norman, to host his own internationally syndicated radio program.

Ryan is absolutely passionate about two things: 1) Offering **H.O.P.E.**, which stands for **H**elping **O**ther **P**eople **E**xcel, and 2) training and competing. "I run

Why Can't We Say What We Mean?

marathons and triathlons for the challenge and feeling you get when you cross the finish line. I want people to see me going after my dreams, in hopes that it inspires them to go after their dreams."

Learn more about Ryan at www.ryancelestain.com and get instant access to "My Web 2.0 Notes" - his FREE 7 step training series on how to brand yourself on the Internet.

INTERVIEW

JED: This is Jed Reay again coming to you with another awesome, awesome interview. Guys, I've got to let you in on this one. This young man is now the up-and-coming thing that we're all looking for, for some direction and guidance. This man is going to speak to us again on communication. This man is an Internet marketer, Internet entrepreneur, and a new up-and-coming radio talk show host, Ryan Celestain from Tulsa, Oklahoma.

Ryan, thank you very, very much for joining us. This project has taken on quite an amazing step here in the last couple of days, and I want to thank you for being a part of the project.

Copyright © 2008. Jed A. Reay. All rights reserved.

RYAN: Jed, thank you so much for allowing me to be a part of the project.

JED: You bet. When we first talked offline before we got this started, this was kind of an amazing transformation about communication. In some respects, the Internet is a nameless, faceless, a very heartless place. When someone sends out an email or sends a message, it's real hard to develop emotion. It's real hard to share what it is that you're thinking or feeling with someone if you don't have open channels of communication.

Let me start off by asking you a couple of questions.

RYAN: Okay, absolutely.

JED: If someone were to ask you, "Ryan, what does it mean to communicate and develop meaningful relationships in a business arena?" what does that mean to you?

RYAN: Be on the same page, on the same level as that other person. For me, it's not really about the money aspects. It's not really about the product. It's about the relationship between the two.

Why Can't We Say What We Mean?

I've been fortunate to meet all different kinds of people with various backgrounds over the last year. It's because I built a relationship, and that was my number one focus.

Communication is a huge, huge part of that. It's very, very important for me in business, because of all the opportunities I've had come from the relationships.

JED: That's amazing, because it really is about what we give first of ourselves to even start a conversation. We start a conversation by being interested in somebody.

That leads me to the next question. How do you know and what cues are you looking at, whether online or offline, on or off your radio show, in the businesses and things that you're going to do, how do you know you've made a connection? What are the keys or the cues that you look at to know that you're making a connection with somebody?

RYAN: Now online, that's sometimes kind of difficult. Offline, for me, you can see sometimes when you make a

Copyright © 2008. Jed A. Reay. All rights reserved.

connection, whether it be eye contact, head movement, body language if someone is receiving the information. It's really easy to tell.

If I'm speaking in front of a group of people or just one-on-one, if they're just nodding just to be nodding and thinking, hopefully, I'm going to quit talking, I can always tell. I can sense that.

On the other hand, if I'm in a group of people and people are actually looking at me, making eye contact with me and smiling, making facial gestures and things like that, I know that they're receiving the information.

Now online, one of the things that's easy for me to pick up on, if I ask someone a question and they don't answer the question, that's a good sign that they're not necessarily involved in the conversation.

One of the things I've experienced is someone will ask me a question in order to pitch me on whatever they want to pitch me on, and I'll answer their question and try to build a relationship with them.

If their response is, "Okay, great" and they pitch me again, that means

Why Can't We Say What We Mean?

> they could care less about building a relationship and talking.
>
> Those are the signs that I look for and the things that I pick up on.

JED: Isn't that the truth? It really is the value of developing a true relationship. This project has provided me with a lot of information from a cross range of very successful people like yourself in the industry, Internet, non-Internet, offline, online.

It's just amazing that when someone is really not engaged with you, and whether you're the one that's initiated the conversation or whether they initiated the conversation, it doesn't really matter.

What does key in is exactly what you said. If they're not taking what you're saying as being a valuable component to move the conversation from A to B, to C, to D, to E, but yet they're still back to their agenda, then you know that's probably not a meaningful conversation.

RYAN: Right.

Copyright © 2008. Jed A. Reay. All rights reserved.

JED: That leads me to the characteristics. Do you think these things are innate, or is this a learned behavior that most people can learn to do; create an effective communication model?

RYAN: I believe people can learn it. We learn everything we do in life. Just like riding a bike, at first it could be kind of difficult. For example, if someone is trying to promote online, their only know-how could be to pitch and sell and say, "Hey, look at my opportunity."

In order for them to become successful, they have to learn. If they don't learn how to communicate and learn how to build relationships, their chances of building a successful business online are slim to none.

JED: I agree. It's interesting, because that leads us to the next question. It's very interesting.

Let's go to that next question, because that's the leap to where you come into this conversation and what's important about what you have to offer.

Can you give our audience maybe a little bit of your advice on how they might improve that interaction or

Why Can't We Say What We Mean?

that communication they might be struggling with?

Let's do something real simple. Say that they need to approach somebody that they feel is very, very important to their life, maybe a significant other, a teacher, their boss, anybody, for that matter, that they put up on a pedestal or see as important. What would you share with our audience as to what they might do?

RYAN: I would say come from the heart. Don't try to be someone you're not. Be yourself and come straight from the heart, because I personally believe that people can sense that.

When you are yourself and you're being who you are, people can sense that it's real, and they know what you're doing or what you're requesting or what you're talking about is real and you believe in it.

I think when people try to act in a way that they are not or throw some hype in there, it becomes fake and it comes across as being fake.

Like I said, just being yourself and coming from the heart, I think people

Copyright © 2008. Jed A. Reay. All rights reserved.

will really get in tune to that and see that.

JED: Cool. You know what, everybody? That came from the heart. I know Ryan, and he means that. I agree. I think that when you come from a position of service, first and foremost, and are truly, truly interested in the other person that you're talking to, you're right. It really is.

Let's talk a little bit about where people can get access to you. Can you give a plug for yourself and what you're doing, the projects you're working on, and just talk a little bit about what you bring to the table?

RYAN: Absolutely. If anyone's interested in learning more about me, they can visit me at www.ryancelestain.com

I'm in an interesting place in my life right now. A year ago, I was a full-time draftsman for a piping company. I absolutely hated it. Fast forward a year later, I love what I'm doing. I'm constantly working on new projects.

The two biggest things that I love and the two biggest things I'm

Why Can't We Say What We Mean?

passionate about are one, offering HOPE. H.O.P.E. stands for Helping Other People Excel. The second thing is training and competing.

I'm a runner. I run marathons. And I'm actually running my first triathlon this year.

JED: Whoo-hoo! All right!

RYAN: I'm extremely excited about that. One of my major, major projects right now is I'm building an internationally syndicated radio show. I'm working with Greg Norman, Sally Jessy Raphael, and Bryant McGill, just to name a few people.

It's a radio program designed towards personal development, personal growth, and just really giving people the tools necessary to go after what they want in life and accomplishing what they want in life.

Those are some of the things that I'm up to right now.

JED: That is totally cool, Ryan. I'll tell you what. We need more spirit in this world. We're all connected. You truly, truly believe in the power of the subconscious and power of the spirit and power of the universe. We need more and more people like yourself bringing the word to the world.

If we realized that we were really, really all tied together, there wouldn't be any more strife and suffering and war and people looking to hurt someone else.

RYAN: Right.

JED: That's really special. I'm proud to know you.

RYAN: Thank you.

JED: You bet. You bet. Let's close this out with a couple of questions that bring this back to the nature of the essence of who you are and what this is all about.

You have some skill. You have some ability to feel and understand and communicate at a very, very high level. What would you suggest that someone does to improve in the area of consciousness, in the area of really fully understanding how to develop a communication

Why Can't We Say What We Mean?

relationship with anyone, but it's directly related to your personal strengths? This is going right to your radio show. This is applied to the personal development.

Let's talk a little bit about that.

RYAN: Personal development, as in communication?

JED: Yes.

RYAN: Okay. It's kind of funny. I'm 24 years old, and in high school I was the shy, quiet guy. I was so shy and so quiet. Everybody knew who I was, but they didn't know anything about me. They just knew that I played sports and I was a pretty good student, and all that stuff.

I was so shy and so quiet. I had to read my senior paper in front of the class. I'm up there and the paper is shaking and my voice is shaking. Sweat is running from every pore in my body and I thought I was going to die.

We fast forward to now, internationally syndicated radio program. I do public speaking engagements for hundreds of people and my videos are all over YouTube.

One thing changed for me, and that's when I was a freshman in college. I was at a point in my life where I had a decision to make. I needed to make some money financially and I didn't care what it was. I had to do what I had to do.

I found a job, I found an opportunity. I was selling knives. It was basically a sales position. I would sit at a kitchen table and talk to a couple for an hour, and I'd get paid $15.

That right there was like, "Okay, wait. You're going to tell me you're going to give me $15 to talk for an hour and I can do as many as I want?"

I said, "Okay."

From then on, I realized that being able to communicate, there's a huge opportunity to do that. I always constantly worked on myself and read different books and tried to plug into different programs just to get better.

It's the same thing with public speaking. I took public speaking

Why Can't We Say What We Mean?

classes in college to get over the fear of speaking in front of people. When other people were scared to death, I was starting to enjoy it. And now, I just look at it as a challenge.

It's the same thing with video. The first time I made a video, it took me two days to make a video, two whole days. And now, I can turn on the camera and five minutes later the video is made. It's just that constant putting myself out there and having the courage to fail, and just learning from my mistakes.

JED: Isn't that the truth? It's a matter of taking action, and T. Harv Eker talks about this. It starts as a thought. Then it becomes a feeling. Then, if you want the result that is at the end, you have to take action.

That's exactly what you did. It became a thought. It became a feeling. That feeling got stronger into an action, and look where you are. Look at the results.

RYAN: Right.

JED: Awesome!

RYAN: Absolutely.

JED: That brings me to the last question, and this is a pretty heavy one.

You are an influential person in the world and becoming more and more influential every single day. I guess the best way to say this is as a teacher, trainer, mentor, human change agent, that's what you are, you have a powerful influence on those of us that come in contact with you.

What do you do to maintain your vision, your direction, your hunger, your thirst, your desire to continue to do what you do? What is it that keeps you jazzed and going every day?

RYAN: I think, for me, it's my running and competing and my training. I can go out and have a hard workout and just put it all on the line. In a way, at times it's kind of therapeutic for me. I can go out for a 22-mile run. And some people are thinking, "What, 22 miles? Three hours of running?"

I'm like, "Oh, yeah!"

I don't run with an iPod. I don't run with anything like that. That's my

Why Can't We Say What We Mean?

time to just kind of think and take everything in. Believe it or not, it's almost relaxing to me. Yeah, I'm putting forth a lot of effort, but it's also just relaxing for me. Once I come home, it's almost like my batteries are recharged and I'm ready to get out there.

When I had my big races, the things that I work hard for, for 6, 9, 12 months, just nonstop training, the big race comes, and when I cross the finish line and I did what I said I was going to do, it's just like, "What's next?"
This last running season was the best running season of my life.

JED: Cool.

RYAN: At the beginning of the season I said, "There are two things I want to accomplish," and at the end of the season, I accomplished both of those two things in the times I said I was going to do it.

For me, the feeling that you get when that happens is priceless.

JED: That's known as that runner's high.

RYAN: Absolutely.

JED: That's really special, Ryan. I've got to tell you, you've been a very special friend in my life before this project even started. We have a very special connection and will for many, many, many years to come. I just really, really thank you for taking the time out of your busy schedule to make this connection to our audience.

That's Ryan Celestain at www.ryancelestain.com

Trust me, you're going to be hearing about this young man for many, many, many years in the future.

We'll call that a wrap. Enjoy.

We look forward to talking to you in the future.

Thank you very much.

Ryan, thanks.

RYAN: Thank you, Jed.

Why Can't We Say What We Mean?

CHAPTER 3: INTERVIEW WITH SETH DALEY

Mr. Seth Daley

Seth Daley, the author and creator of ProBusinessReviews.com and HomeBusinessTrafficMasters.com, is a home business entrepreneur and Internet marketer who believes in the power of contribution.

Seth comes from a sales background of six years in the telecommunications industry, where he was able to test and develop his communication skills that enabled him to achieve the top 10% in sales. For the past three years, Seth has been teaching, coaching, and training new Internet entrepreneurs in the art of instant credibility, lead generation, and Web 2.0 technology.

Seth believes that the first step to **improving the quality of business communication** is to really understand where the other person is coming from, to put yourself in the other person's shoes. Seth says, "When you have an understanding and put yourself in their shoes, then you can truly begin the communication process."

Visit www.sethdaley.com for more information, and get Seth's FREE video that reveals 7 highly

www.jedthecommunicator.com

effective, low-cost methods to boost your business in 90 days or less at www.homebusinesstrafficmasters.com

INTERVIEW

JED: Hello. It's Jed Reay again, and I come to you with another fascinating interview for this book, *Why Can't We Say What We Mean? Developing Meaningful Business Relationships Through Effective Communication.*

I'm sitting here having the privilege of introducing Seth Daley. Seth is an Internet marketer and past corporate salesperson, who brings a lot of attention to detail to this project.

I'm so thankful, Seth, that you took the time out of your busy schedule to talk to us.

SETH: Absolutely. It's my pleasure, Jed. I really appreciate you taking the time to talk about communication. That's what we're here to do.

JED: It's interesting. This project has taken on quite a life of its own. It's very interesting how this has all transpired. You were some of the

Why Can't We Say What We Mean?

catalyst for this and I have to thank you.

The whole premise was this dichotomy between faceless, nameless websites, emails, technology, and it didn't seem to me like it was improving communication.

I'll ask you, in your opinion, in a business environment, how do you improve the quality of your communication?

SETH: The first thing that I would say, Jed, to improve your business communication is to really understand where the other person is coming from.

When you have an understanding and put yourself in their shoes, then you can truly begin that communication process. There are certain things that you can do to be able to flip the tables. We can talk about that as the interview progresses, but really it's putting yourself in their shoes or on the other side of the table.

JED: Right, thank you. The whole point of communication is trying and working towards a common goal in

Copyright © 2008. Jed A. Reay. All rights reserved.

the relationship. The only way that you can do that is by putting them first.

In the communication mechanism of creating effective business communication, there are some skill sets. Let me ask you. Do you think that we were born with these skill sets, or is this something that can be learned?

SETH: Absolutely, it can be learned. We're all born with different backgrounds. We have different parents, different cultures, different societies, and different influences.

But one thing, when you begin to learn the communication process and begin to understand communication, your background doesn't have anything to do with the ability to communicate, once you learn a set of skills.

You can absolutely learn to communicate.

JED: It's that fear factor that a lot of people think that they can't speak well or can't communicate well, or they can't carry on a conversation. But you've made it your career to do that.

Why Can't We Say What We Mean?

It's interesting. You're working on a project right now, which is helping people to connect with other people, helping people to connect with like minds, as well as other people that might not even realize that they exist.

Do you want to talk about that project and what you're working on?

SETH: Absolutely. We're in the Internet age right now, and the one obstacle that people have when they have a business opportunity or a small business is connecting with people.

There's a new trend, which is Web 2.0. Web 2.0 is user-generated content, user-generated information. You've got sites out there like Facebook, MySpace, and YouTube that really close the gap in communication.

Ten years ago or a couple of years ago, if I wanted to be face-to-face with you, I'd have to be physically in your presence.

Now, because of technology we can actually close that gap. I can be on a video and you can be on a video. We can see eye-to-eye and still have that

Copyright © 2008. Jed A. Reay. All rights reserved.

effective communication. You can read body language. You can begin to form a relationship with each other.

Like with YouTube, you can have a video out there. People can begin to know you, like you, and trust you just by using that technology. You don't even have to be there.

It begins the communication process. You can use technology too. You can use technology to hide behind, or you can use technology to project yourself.

JED: That's right. That's what's really interesting. I'm a little bit older than you, Seth, but I spent many, many, many years in that face-to-face interaction. Computers weren't available, or at a high enough tech at that point. We didn't see a lot of this Web 2.0 technology. We didn't see a lot of the whole Internet social networking, bookmarking, or the interaction. We didn't see that.

The only way that you were going to connect with people was face to face. I agree with you, Seth, that it has opened up a great avenue of access and made it international.

Why Can't We Say What We Mean?

My contention when I started this was that it was impersonal, but I agree with you. The more I've gotten into this process and interviewing very select people through this book process, I have to say I've had to back pedal a little bit.

I do agree that it can, but there has to be an effort made in order to do that.

Let me ask you just this. In terms of the communication style, and let's talk about Web 2.0., what are you looking for in someone when you know that you're making a connection with them? How do you know you're making a connection?
Talk a little bit about maybe some of the features that are used. Say there is somebody that gives a video response to you, or that they give an email response, or they bookmark it, or something to that effect.

Let's talk about that as being the triggers. Tell me a little bit about the triggers that make you know that you've connected with these people.

SETH: There are a couple of different ways. Obviously, the number one thing is response. Are people responding to your video? Are they responding to your message?

If you have a targeted message towards a targeted audience, you're most likely going to get a response back, whether it's negative or positive. It doesn't matter as long as you are getting a response back.

It's absolutely the response. When you get enough responses back, you can see if you're on the right trail, if you're hitting, striking, or penetrating your core message, whatever that is, to your targeted audience.

JED: Interesting. That brings me to the series of end questions. This whole process of being in front of people, of being part of a leadership role, that's what you find yourself in. You're in a leadership role there, and that's pretty intense.

For some of the people that don't have this experience, can you tell us a little bit about where they're going to get some of this information? Give us some tidbits about maybe how they can improve their Web 2.0 situation or their communication, and where they can get a hold of you?

Why Can't We Say What We Mean?

SETH: I might take a little bit different route than what the question is. The tool that everybody can use when you don't have, maybe, the leadership role, you don't have the experience down, the number one thing you can do is contribute to people's lives.

What I mean by that is the language that we're all speaking is our own language, and it's our own experiences. Like you said at first, if you can flip the table and put yourself in their shoes and then look for opportunities to serve that person, you can contribute to their lives. Essentially what's going to happen is the dynamic of the conversation is going to change.

The dynamic of the relationship is going to change. When you give of yourself freely, whatever or not it comes back from this person, it doesn't matter, the doors are going to be opened. It's all through contribution that you contribute.

You'll see in any of my videos, you'll see in any of my emails that go out, in any of my interaction with my database, with my clients, with my customers, you're going to see an element of contribution. Everything I do I put in an element that's useful for them, information they can take and improve their life, improve their business.

That's the number one tool.

Here's another thing. If you don't think you have anything to offer, go out and get educated. There are numerous sites out there where you can just read free information. At www.ezinearticles.com you can find anything you want on a subject and you can become educated in just a few hours.

JED: That's very, very good advice, Seth. Thank you.

I do want you to touch on your website and where people can come to meet you and get in contact with you.

SETH: Absolutely, two places are www.sethdaley.com and also my new product that is launching shortly here at www.homebusinesstrafficmasters.com

If you're in the arena, or if you're looking to enhance your Web 2.0

Why Can't We Say What We Mean?

	skills, or if you're learning how to drive traffic to your site, but also want to make it relationship based with your targeted audience, then www.homebusinesstrafficmasters.com is the place to go.
JED:	Traffic Masters, that really says a lot about Seth and what his goal is for helping other people. That was the key thing that he said, providing value and giving value to others first.
	That brings me to this final question. When we do that, it takes a lot out of us. We provide our spirit, our soul, our heart, and everything that we do we do first and foremost for someone else. How do you keep yourself jazzed? How do you keep yourself charged with energy and wanting to keep coming back when some of the people that we communicate with require a lot more of our attention, a lot more of our effort to help them through some hurdles?
	It takes a lot of energy. What do you do to fill yourself, fill your tank?
SETH:	It's important to take that time. This is a way that I do it, and it's just one word. It's called "gratefulness." What I mean by that is that every day

I wake up, and multiple times throughout the day I stop and I just feel grateful for what I have.

Even if the day isn't going well, I still have things to be grateful for. Things are going around in our lives on a daily basis. You may have lost a sale, had a refund request, or something comes up in your personal life and takes you away from your business.

If you stop and you just notice what is in your life around you. For me, I have a beautiful wife. I have two kids that love me. I could stop right there and start feeling good.

JED: Right, family is everything.

SETH: But for people who may not have that, you have to keep looking. You're still breathing. You might live in a great country. You might have a support network around you. You may know how to speak and write. You may have the eyes to see this video. You may have the eyes and the ability to read and learn something new.

Anybody can come up with something if you look hard enough, if you just take notice of all the

Why Can't We Say What We Mean?

things that we have in life. That's what fills me up on a daily basis and gets me excited, being grateful.

When you're grateful, it actually opens up other opportunities in your life. I teach a lot about gratefulness. You can go to my website and find out about the *15 Minute Miracle Method*, which has transformed lives.

JED: It has. I can speak personally to that. The *15 Minute Miracle* is a very special time in my morning ritual, every single morning. I will tell you, it has transformed everything that I do and everything that I believe in.

Seth, I just thank you so much for the time that you gave to this project, to me personally, and I just have to tell you, I love you, brother.

SETH: I love you too, Jed. Thank you so much.

JED: You bet.

CHAPTER 4: INTERVIEW WITH KATRINA FERGUSON

Ms. Katrina Ferguson

Katrina Ferguson is a **Master Trainer** who has coached and mentored women around the world through her **Total Woman Workshop** presentations. She delivers a passionate, enthusiastic, and entertaining message to both teach and encourage you to celebrate your individuality and break through to become your "greater self." Her inspiring message is based upon lessons learned in her own breakthrough journeys, and she is committed to helping others across the world apply these principles in their individual lives and relationships.

In her unique and uncompromising style, she brings life-changing principles and leadership skills that have inspired and motivated thousands across age, gender, and industry lines. As such, Katrina has been the subject of numerous articles and

Why Can't We Say What We Mean?

interviews, and her story is currently being used all over the country to train and motivate sales forces of both public and private organizations.

She routinely shares the stage with company presidents and executives as she conducts training and presentations around the country.

Visit www.thetotalwomanworkshop.com to learn more about Katrina and her **Total Woman Workshop** for breakthroughs in every area of your life.

INTERVIEW

JED: Good morning, everyone. This is Jed Reay coming to you with another awesome, awesome interview. I have the privilege of speaking with and interviewing Katrina Ferguson.

Katrina delivers a passionate, enthusiastic, and entertaining message to both teach and encourage you to celebrate your individuality and break through to become your greater self. She delivers inspiring messages. These messages are based on lessons that she has learned in her own breakthrough journeys.

Katrina, welcome.

Copyright © 2008. Jed A. Reay. All rights reserved.

www.jedthecommunicator.com

KATRINA: Thank you. Thank you for having me, Jed.

JED: You know, when we first came in contact with one another, we were chatting about this project and about creating conversation with someone. The book title, of course, is *Why Can't We Say What We Mean? Developing Meaningful Business Relationships Through Effective Communication*

Of all the people that I have come in contact with regarding to this project, they have all shared with me some of their very personal insights. That's what we're going to do today.

Katrina, what does it mean to you to develop meaningful relationships in your business arena?

KATRINA: For me, Jed, meaningful relationships in business are not that different than they are personally. The bottom line is, in any type of communication, you're trying to create a connection. It's kind of a place where you can both meet that forms a foundation that you can build off of.

Anytime that you're communicating with someone, the first thing you

Why Can't We Say What We Mean?

want to do is find a commonality, something that you have in common that allows that connection to take place, so that now you can communicate more deeply.

JED: Interesting. Yes, I would agree. Isn't it interesting that the common theme here is that common ground, so that there is a sense of meaning?

In your opinion, assuming that this is not innate behavior, what characteristics or abilities does one need to be an effective communicator?

KATRINA: To become an effective communicator, you need to take hold of some principles and philosophies and things that I've learned from some of my mentors. Of course, we just talked about the connection piece, but the other part being understanding that over 70% of communication is in the body language. It's in what you can see that's not really being said through the mouth.

That's why emails, text messaging, and all of the ways that we communicate currently, we call it high-tech communication, is not even really communication. It's almost just sharing information. There's not really any communication.

It's very difficult to send an emotion via email, a certain type of glance or a certain type of a movement that really lets you know that the other person is understanding where you're coming from.

Clearly, I can't tell you how many times I've had to explain an email because someone read it in a tone differently than I actually wrote it. We have to be very, very conscious that when we're communicating nonverbally, to express in writing the nonverbal communication part to create and maintain that connection.

It's simpler when you're face to face and you can actually see the body language and the responses, so you can read not just what they're saying, but actually how they're responding to what it is that they're saying.

There's a book out there called *Never Be Lied To Again*. It deals specifically with understanding body movements so that you can tell when someone is not communicating honestly and in a forthcoming

Why Can't We Say What We Mean?

fashion. That's basically what we're doing anytime that we're talking face to face and we're getting an impression of one another.

I know in sales, as a sales trainer, one of the things that I teach people to do is to win friends in 30 seconds or less. Of course, we know that's the book by Dale Carnegie, *How To Win Friends and Influence People*. That's very basic to the communication process, learning how to make a friend. If you can do it in 30 seconds or less, then you're that much further ahead in your communication.

In the sales process I teach them to find something about that person that you can comment on, that you can compliment them on. In complimenting them, you start that communication slow. Then you can begin to ask questions. As you're asking questions, then you get to know about that person, and then you can completely ask even more questions. That's how you keep the communication going.

It's the funniest thing. I've seen this happen even recently when I was introduced to a gentleman by one of my friends. In our initial conversation, all I did was ask him questions, and he did all the talking in the entire conversation.

Afterwards, when he got off the phone with me, he went back to my friend and said, "Wow! I really like her."

He knows absolutely nothing about me, other than my name and what I do, because I asked so many questions that he talked about himself.

When you're trying to win friends and influence people, you want them to like you, and you do that by continuing to ask them questions. A lot of times people just need someone to hear them, to listen, to care enough.

The next step would be to mirror and match even their body language. If they're standing with their arms crossed on their chest, then you cross your arms across your chest. It's almost like copying everything that they do, in terms of their body.
They won't necessarily notice that that's what you're doing, but they'll walk away with, "You know, there's

Why Can't We Say What We Mean?

something about that person that I really like."

It's simply the fact that you mirror and match them. They feel comfortable with you and there's a connection. It makes it easier for them to receive the sales process of whatever communication it is or connection you're trying to establish.

JED: Isn't that fascinating? It really, truly is that simple. In that time that you just gave me, it answered several of the other questions that I had for you. It's interesting, because I didn't need to ask them. That is just amazing to me.

I do have quite an interesting question here. What would you consider to be your personal strength in the arena of communication? You've given some characteristics and some abilities and ideas about what transpires in a conversation, but what about you personally?

KATRINA: Personally, I believe one of my strengths, and this is just evident by what people say when they've left my presence, or when people have been introduced to me, or whatnot, is that when people walk away they know I really care.

Somehow I'm able to convey in my body language, in my conversation, in my tone, my facial expressions that they're important to me. People are important to me.

That's my burning desire. That's what God put me here to do, is to effect change in the lives of people. Communicating that with my body language and, of course, with my verbal skills without really saying, "I care about you," is a strong suit.

People don't really care how much you know until they know how much you care. That just goes all the way back to the initial question. How do you communicate and make the connections so that people trust you, believe you, and know that you've got their best interest at heart?

JED: Right, right.

KATRINA: That's where you can begin to get some inspiration going. The inspiration causes them to be motivated entirely, and it's the motivation that causes them to move further ahead than they would have,

Why Can't We Say What We Mean?

	had you not been involved in the process.
JED:	Sure.
KATRINA:	I get that question about motivation so often. How do you motivate your team? How do you motivate your children? How do you motivate anyone? You really can't do that.
	Just by virtue of the definition of motivation, you have to move yourself.
JED:	Right.
KATRINA:	All we can do is inspire someone to move.
JED:	Yes.
KATRINA:	You do that by understanding who they are, finding out what their purpose is, why they are here, and then you eliminate that "why" for them. Then they figure out how to do it and go out there and get it done.
JED:	Amen.
KATRINA:	That's why, if you notice everywhere, in my bios and on my website, it says, "If your *why* is big

enough, the *how* will take care of itself."

JED: It's so true. That is so true. It's a visual thing. Right this moment, we're doing this remotely. I'm not in my home studio. I'm at T. Harv Eker's Millionaire Mind Intensive in Seattle, Washington right now.

It's really, really interesting how the whole vision thing is so critical. The communications that are taking place where I am currently are quite fascinating, because you can tell who's connected, who's connecting, and who's not connecting just because of what you just said about their why, number one.

Secondly, because of body posture, because of something going on in the room they're not attentive. Their eye contact isn't there, for whatever reason.

That leads me to my next question, and then into more of a bigger discussion about what you're doing for the rest of the world.

Is there something that you can give our audience, maybe a tidbit that can help them develop a better communication skill or skills? Talk a

Why Can't We Say What We Mean?

                    little bit about your Total Woman Workshop and what you're currently doing right now.

KATRINA: Absolutely. I know from the front room, whether you're training, teaching, inspiring, there are certain things that I always keep in mind, in terms of my audience.

The easiest way to describe how I do this is we have to find a way or mode, if you will, to connect with every single person in that room at some level. Sometimes you'll look out and you'll see people are wandering; they're not really paying attention. You have to know how to pull them back. You need to know how to keep them engaged.

One of the best ways that I've found to teach how to engage every single member of your audience is to make sure that you address them by personality types. We believe that most people fall into some combination of four personality types, and we designate them by the four fish, for instance.

JED: Right.

KATRINA: We say that an urchin, they just want to know the facts. They want to

Copyright © 2008. Jed A. Reay. All rights reserved.

know the statistics. They want to know the numbers, the information.

A whale is just concerned about how this information allows him to help people. How can he use this to go out and assist the masses?

The dolphins, they want to have fun. "Show me the party in the opportunity. Show me how I can put on my little red dress and hang out with some people and build relationships."

Finally, the shark's personality type is motivated by the money and the ability to make more. "How can I create more money, maybe invest more money by the information that you're sharing?" When you're speaking, you want to make sure you talk about the money so the shark is engaged. When you're talking about the information, the shark may or may not be paying any attention.

JED: Sure.

KATRINA: If you can build your presentation so that you address all four personality types at different points in your presentation, then everybody will walk away saying, "Wow! I got something from that."

Why Can't We Say What We Mean?

And when you mix that with humor, it's funny. I was telling somebody that the other day. I said, "You know, when I was broke I wasn't funny in front of the room, because not being able to feed your kids was absolutely no joke."

JED: Sure.

KATRINA: But to be able to go from barely being able to feed your children to making over six figures from home in a three-year period of time, now all of a sudden life is a little happier. There's a little more levity in that.

That's really how we make sure from the front of the room that we're connecting with everyone and making sure that everyone leaves with something from our presentation. We use that. We actually teach that during the Total Woman Workshop.

We do those all around the country, where we bring in women and men who have women in their lives, whether that woman is their mother, their sister, or their wives. We bring them in and we teach them how to communicate, how to become total

www.jedthecommunicator.com

and whole in every area of your life. Whether it's your face, your fitness, your finances, your focus, whatever it is, we help them to become whole.

As a matter of face, the next workshop is June 21st in Atlanta, Georgia. We just came from Harrisburg, Pennsylvania. Over the summer, we'll be doing Vegas, Philadelphia, and New York.

All of that information, of course, is available at the website www.thetotalwomanworkshop.com

Additionally, the workshop will present other types of events as well, other types of seminars. The Total Woman Workshop is actually a seminar company.

For instance, we just did the "Total Woman Workshop Presents Breakthrough To Your Wealthy Place," featuring the world's only breakthrough speaker, "Dr. Breakthrough" himself, Dr. Stan Harris.

That's really what we're doing. We've been doing the workshops locally here in the Maryland area for the last couple of years, but this year

Why Can't We Say What We Mean?

we've released it on the road. People's lives are being changed.

We're just really, really fortunate that this is the vehicle that was used to help us bring change to the masses.

JED: It's really interesting. You said something that I want to address and come back to, which is an extremely powerful vision for me. It's a very powerful vision for a lot of people that we come in contact with.

You made a comment about needing to feed your kids, needing to take care of your children, needing to support your family. There was a point in your life that it didn't look good. But you had a vision and you had a direction and you had a burning desire. You had an answer and a conclusion, and look where you are today because of your strength, because of your direction, your drive, your desire to not stay where you were.

That leads me, basically, to the final question. As a teacher, trainer, mentor, human change agent, you have a powerful influence on those of us that you work with. What is it that you do to maintain that vision, that direction, hunger, that desire to keep going?

KATRINA: There's one thing I learned very early, and that is I had to be clear about my priorities. Anytime I make a decision to do anything, I run it through a mental list of priorities that I actually have posted in my office.

What this does is it helps to keep me on purpose, living on purpose and doing destiny. One of the things that I teach is that everybody was created. When God created us, he had something specific in mind; from problems that we were specifically created to solve, from who the people that we were specifically created to assist and to build up.

If we can both find out what that why is, focus on the why, separate ourselves from the challenges that will come to keep you from living life on purpose, then we can actually do what we were created to do. That's when you find your passion. That's where you're able to make a change.

I teach people how to find their why. I help them to determine what the

Why Can't We Say What We Mean?

challenges are that keep them from living their why and doing their why. I help them to figure out what their IQ is to make sure that their 'I Quit' is "I will until," so that they realize that this is a lifetime of living and not just a season of living that we're going to go through.

We take that and begin to apply it to our lives and our priorities. I know first and foremost, if what I'm being asked to do goes against what I believe God has called me to do, I won't do it.

I have my first priorities. When I have a spouse, I don't have one right now, but that will be my next priority after God. Then comes my family, and beyond that, my physical fitness, and finally, my business endeavors.

When anyone asks me to do anything I run it through that list. If there's a conflicting demand, I know right up front with clarity what I need to do. I decided previously.

The root of the word decide is "cide," which means to kill other options. You only hear it in a few words, like homicide and infanticide. When you kill all other options and you say, "Okay, I'm going to live on purpose and I'm going to make decisions based on this," and then you do it with discipline, nothing can stop you.

I mean, literally, I went from grocery shopping in my mother's pantry, from showing up at my girlfriends' houses with my three kids around dinnertime hoping somebody would feed us, to now being able to focus on feeding the nation.

Why? Because I figured out what my why was, what my purpose was, and I didn't allow the situation or circumstances of life to stop me from reaching those goals, from doing it.

Have I achieved all of it? No, but I'm steadily on my way. You don't ever fail until you stop moving.

JED: Wow, Katrina! I just can't tell you how that just made me feel. You know, it is so, so true. You know what? I don't know if I have anymore comment to that. There's no way that I can speak. Thank you.

Thank you so very much for the time that you've given. That was a very, very special time for me and for our audience.

Why Can't We Say What We Mean?

KATRINA: Thank you for having me. I appreciate it.

JED: You bet. Thank you very much. We'll call that a wrap.

CHAPTER 5:
INTERVIEW WITH KANDEE G

Ms. Kandee G

Kandee G is an internationally recognized speaker, life coach and author who believes a remarkable life is available to us all and gives us the keys to **release the imprisoned splendor**. She walks us through the process to realize the things about us that we don't see for ourselves.

Her coaching provides guidance and self-management that has empowered thousands to navigate through the turbulent storms of life. Kandee pulls from her own hardships, setbacks, and challenging experiences as a single mother who went from peanut butter to being transported by private jets.

Why Can't We Say What We Mean?

Audiences are amazed with Kandee's strategic thinking and winning approach. They have gained not only from her speeches and seminars, but also from her celebrated life coaching program **G.A.M.E.S., A Pathway to Personal Action**.

Get your copy of Kandee's newly released *Now Boarding: Next Stop - Your Remarkable Life* and learn more about living the life others only dream about, available at www.kandeeg.com

INTERVIEW

JED: Good morning, everyone. I'd like to introduce a very special guest, someone that is going to share with us her insights and benefits to our project, *Why Can't We Say What We Mean? Developing Meaningful Business Relationships Through Effective Communication*.

I'd like to welcome Kandee G. She can be heard on WKAT radio from 11:00 a.m. to 12:00 p.m. on Mondays and Thursdays in South Florida. Kandee G, welcome.

KANDEE: Thank you so much, Jed. I'm really happy to be here with you.

JED: Listen, Kandee, the reason that you and I came to know one another was in a referral from a mutual friend of

Copyright © 2008. Jed A. Reay. All rights reserved.

ours. It's interesting how this project has grown and grown and grown and grown, and just opened the doors to very special people.

You come with an interesting pedigree of background, and I'd like to start off by asking you a few questions that directly relate to this book and the audience that'll be reading this or listening to this or watching it.

If someone were to ask you, "What does it mean to communicate and develop a meaningful relationship in a business arena?" what does that mean to you?

KANDEE: I actually think, Jed, it means everything. I think relationships in all aspects are absolutely everything. When we can truly learn to first have a real relationship with our self, understand who we are so that we can be completely and totally wholly authentic, then there are things that we can do as we move on into the business arena.

Jed, it's true in the personal arena, where we can begin to help create the things that we want in our life, based on who we are in an authentic way, but also being able to relate to

Why Can't We Say What We Mean?

>other folks and attract those people to us that we want to have in our life.
>
>I said a whole mouthful there.

JED: That's interesting because it does lead me right to the second question.

>When you're having a conversation with someone, or a group of people, what is it that you cue into, or what is it that you see or feel or experience that lets you know that you're making a connection with that person or a group of people?

KANDEE: A lot of that has to do with the way I feel, my own intuition. Also, things like obvious things, like eye contact and body language. I rely a lot on my own intuition and my own internal wisdom. I've spent a lot of time, Jed, in real self-discovery and understanding what's important to me.

>The other piece of that is I'm always looking to see what's important to you. When I'm in a conversation, it's like, "What is important to you?" There's a place where I know we connect there. It goes back to being authentic and true and knowing what it is that you want.

The truth is, as you focus on those things that you want and can continue to stay focused there, you'll begin to draw people and situations to you that allow that to come to you a lot more easily and a lot more effortlessly.

With that being said, learning how to tap into your own intuition, but also learning how to find out what's important to someone else, you can really make a true connection.

JED: Isn't that amazing? It seems like without even having any collaboration between all the participants in this book, that that seems to be the common theme.
The next question really is rather moot, because I set it up as a question.

What characteristics or personalities or abilities does someone need to be an effective communicator, assuming that it's not innate? I make the assumption that it's not. When the doctor slaps our fanny and we cry, that doesn't mean that we're a born communicator. It's a learned behavior. Can you address some of those?

Why Can't We Say What We Mean?

KANDEE: Absolutely. I think one of the things that makes somebody a great communicator is when somebody can truly, truly be a good listener. See, oftentimes folks are hearing but not listening. People are busy running so many tapes inside their head that oftentimes they're not hearing what someone else is truly saying.

In order to be a real effective communicator, you need to be present, you need to pay attention, and you need to listen.

JED: I think that's why the good Lord gave us two ears and one mouth, huh? Can you give our audience some simple steps to improve their abilities to communicate and connect with someone?

KANDEE: One thing that I would say is an extraordinarily effective tool is learning to meditate every day. You might say, "What does meditation have to do with communication?"

When we can truly learn how to clear our minds and allow ourselves to be present in the moment, we can truly become great, effective communicators.

Copyright © 2008. Jed A. Reay. All rights reserved.

One great tool which does much, much more than help to effect great communication, and it does a whole lot more for your life, is truly learning how to meditate.

I'm not saying, "Oh, yeah, I've done that meditation thing." I'm talking sitting down for 15 or 20 minutes every day, getting to stillness, emptying your mind and making it a practice. A byproduct of that will really help effect great communication.

Beyond that is learning how to be a conscious, free, deliberate thinker, paying attention to the thoughts coming in, so that when you're responding, you're responding within the environment that you're communicating in.

Another thing that I might say about the person you're communicating with is to really learn what's important to them.

JED: Wow, that was a mouthful! Thank you. I really appreciate that. That then leads me to this next point.

You offer services, a product, skills, training, mentoring, coaching,

Why Can't We Say What We Mean?

whatever adjective you want to use to identify the product and service portfolio that you have. Can you give our audience some insight and direction of where they might go to get some assistance from you?

KANDEE: In order to effect change in our own life, and let's face it, Jed, it all begins with us, our lives are our responsibility. In order to effect real change, one of the key aspects of that is being able to spend some time in real personal discovery, really spending time with you to uncover the things that are important to you, how you got the things that you didn't want and how to begin to define what you do want.

One of the things that I know to be true is oftentimes when folks come to me for coaching or mentoring, they come to me with this, "I don't know what I want out of life. All I know is that I'm not fulfilled and I'm not happy. I'm not getting what I want, but I don't know what that is."

That comes through personal discovery and self-review. That is absolutely a key aspect. Beyond that, it's beginning to understand. We've heard it all before; thoughts are things, think and grow rich, our thoughts create our reality.

The truth is that people need to truly understand that everything in our lives is affected by the way we think in our conscious and our unconscious thinking, and truly, when it comes to our unconscious thinking, how important that is.

Ninety-six percent of our behavior is a direct result of our non-conscious thought. What that means is until you can begin to understand what's happening there, and then devise systems to get your thinking on track and to stay focused on what you want after you've uncovered that. This is part of the direction that I teach folks.

JED: Oh, my land. I just had one of those ah-has. We had not spent a whole lot of time communicating before we had this interview. I have got to say I am truly blessed. This project is truly blessed. Thank you very, very much for speaking consciousness about what we are, what we're trying to accomplish, and what we are accomplishing.

Thank you. That was awesome.

Copyright © 2008. Jed A. Reay. All rights reserved.

Why Can't We Say What We Mean?

KANDEE: You're welcome.

JED: I just started sitting with Steven Sadleir of the Self Awareness Institute in California about five weeks ago, and my life has taken an entirely different path than I ever imagined for myself.

It is truly, truly peaceful and blessed. It's just amazing how things have progressed in my life. I'm on the same page.

Let's direct ourselves back to kind of a final question that will then maybe generate some more conversation with you.

Finally, as a teacher, trainer, mentor, human change agent, you have a very powerful influence on those of us that you come in contact with. What do you do to maintain your vision, direction, thirst, hunger, desire, and to continue?

It is extremely draining the human energy, this pace we're on, the things that you do, the contacts we have. Unfortunately, people come to us with a lot of negative energy. What is it that you do to maintain that focus?

KANDEE: One of the things that I will tell you, Jed, is that I truly live a life of service. I really believe that I've been gifted with this information so that I can make a difference in the lives of others. There's a place where I so understand that, that I'm grounded in my beliefs.

I will tell you also, I talked about meditation earlier. I can't talk enough about it. I meditate every day. It's extraordinarily grounding.

In addition to that, I've engineered ways to keep my thinking on track. I have systems that I put into place that I can plug into whenever I need to. As a matter of fact, it's part of what I teach, because we all need to find ways to keep our thinking on track.

Jesus said, "Be ye not conformed to this world, but be ye transformed by the renewing of your mind." I know, because I've been studying thought transformation for well over 30 years how important it is to keep my thinking on track.

I've set up systems so that I do that every day, every day. I just make sure every single day that I'm out

Why Can't We Say What We Mean?

living what my purpose is. I make sure that every day I touch someone's life in a positive and productive way, because I know that's what I'm meant to do.

JED: That leads me into letting everyone know that they can get a hold of you at www.kandeeg.com
Your comment leads to this vision program. Do you want to speak a little bit about what this is? I'm on your site right now looking at The Vision Program.

KANDEE: I have a coaching program and a mentoring program. Several years ago, I wrote the program to be able to take it inside a bigger arena, like corporate arenas or bigger organizations.

I actually go in and do exactly what I talked to you about. I help folks inside a bigger place understand how they're getting what they don't want in a collective way, how to define what it is that they do want in a collective way, a co-vision, a shared vision, and teach them about values and shared vision and shared values.

I teach them how to engineer the same systems to help keep their

	thinking on track. I help to put entire groups of folks and organizations on track in the same direction to some pretty extraordinary results, I'm very proud to say.
JED:	It looks like it. I'm looking at this website and I'm very, very impressed.
KANDEE:	Thank you.
JED:	Kandee, I can't begin to thank you enough for your involvement in this project. I look forward to sharing with you more and more in the future. I know that our audience will definitely benefit from your involvement. I'd like to thank you very much for your time, Kandee, and we'll talk to you again soon.
KANDEE:	All right. Thank you. Bye for now.

Why Can't We Say What We Mean?

CHAPTER 6:
INTERVIEW WITH
DR. FRAN HARRIS

Dr. Fran Harris

Dr. Fran Harris is a **WNBA Champion**, business strategist and coach, radio and TV personality, author, fitness expert, inspirational speaker and life coach. She knows how to inspire, teach, and transform people in a way that honors where they are, yet challenges them to move in the direction of their wildest dreams.

She knew at an early age that her calling was to touch the lives of millions of people through her spiritually-centered ministry that focuses on **empowerment, entrepreneurship, and service**.

Fran has traveled to over 30 countries, played professional basketball in Italy and Switzerland, and has endured her own share of highlights and lowlights, including being on NCAA (University of

Texas at Austin) and WNBA Championship (Houston Comets) teams, and losing her mother at age 16. These and other experiences give Fran a powerful and unique perspective on human potential.

Get Fran's motivational books and CDs and learn more about this dynamic leader at www.franharris.com where you can also book her for your next live event.

INTERVIEW

JED: Hello and good evening. I have a special guest on the line, Dr. Fran Harris. Dr. Fran Harris is one of those well-behaved women rarely making history. That's the motto for which Fran Harris lives her life.

A WNBA champion, NCAA champion, and Olympic Team Alternate, Fran has traveled more than 30 countries spreading the enthusiastic message of possibility and prosperity.

She is a talk show host and former ESPN announcer whose company recently launched *Collegepreneur*, the first entrepreneurship magazine for college students. The author of more than 14 books, Fran currently coaches and consults clients,

Why Can't We Say What We Mean?

including solo-entrepreneurs and emerging business and fortune 20 corporations whose revenues top $1 trillion.

Dr. Fran, welcome.

FRAN: Good to be here, great to be here. Thank you for having me, Jed.

JED: It is truly a pleasure. It's one of those kinds of projects that has evolved in the course of the last two and one-half weeks. This thing has just grown into an amazing project.

Basically, what Fran and I are doing here is having a conversation about this book, *Why Can't We Say What We Mean? Developing Meaningful Business Relationships Through Effective Communication*, and ultimately, about having conversations.

That being said, Fran, let me ask you a question. What does that mean to you? What does it mean to communicate and create a meaningful relationship in the business arena?

FRAN: First, I have to say I am especially enthusiastic about this topic, and it's so wonderful that somehow we entered into each other's space. I'm working with a couple of clients, multi-billion dollar clients I might add, right now who are being challenged with exactly what you're talking about.

One of the things that I'm working with them on is having a greater level of authenticity in their communication within their company, and when I heard what you were doing, you have no idea how excited I got. I thought, "This is it! This is exactly what I'm trying to get these senior level people and vice presidents and chairmen of companies to get."

That we have to start to interact and communicate at a completely different level if you want to have, a) a good working environment, and b) continue to be profitable with the bottom line.

People are finally starting to see that there is a line, that there is a correlation between healthy, enriching, honest, authentic communication in the business place and a great lifestyle within that same business environment.

Why Can't We Say What We Mean?

	I am thrilled to be talking about this. It's very important to me. It means everything to me.
JED:	You rock, I love it. It's true. It really, truly is. We have come, I think, to a precipice. We have come to this point where we're standing on the cliff and there's a decision to make of whether or not we're going to fall off and fall apart, or whether we're going to stand strong and stand for conviction, belief, our spirit, our attitude, and all of those kinds of things.
	Hey, welcome to the call. I love this. This is great.
	Let's start a dialogue. That dialogue is what kind of components do you see that are critical for having a meaningful conversation in a business environment?
FRAN:	I think the first thing is there has to be an incredible level of accountability. Accountability is one of those words that people throw around kind of like talent, kind of like opportunity, just words that people use and people go, "Ah!"

But when you really look at accountability and you talk about communicating effectively in the business place, you're talking about a couple of things.

One of the things I talk to my clients about is when you're sharing something in the business place, a) you have to not make it personal, and b) the person on the other end has to not take it personally.

There is a sheer talent and a sheer craft to saying what needs to be said, that's honesty and integrity without making it a personal attack. One of the things that really impedes great communication in any relationship is this feeling that somebody's out to get us, this notion that something's behind the word.

We all talk about the meeting after the meeting. What I'm trying to get my clients to do is say, "Let's just say it and honor people in the moment. Be honest, and then we don't have to have the meeting after the meeting. We don't have to say things afterwards that we wouldn't say to those people."

There is a great level of accountability, but there is also the

Why Can't We Say What We Mean?

commitment to truly saying what you mean in the moment. The reason people don't do it, and maybe we're going to get to this, but one of the reasons people don't do it is that they have all kinds of fears about what's going to happen "if I'm really honest, if I really tell people how I feel."

There's been a bad experience with a lot of us, because whenever somebody says, "Oh, she just tells it the way it is," we always think that it is rude or it's mean, but t doesn't have to be.

One of the things I even work with my coaching clients on is let's practice saying what is important to be said without taking personal digs at people, without having to be passive-aggressive. I see a lot of that in corporate America and in relationships in general, because people are afraid of what's going to happen. "I have to get my digs in somehow."

JED: Isn't that something?

FRAN: And getting people to let go, quite frankly, of the ego's need for digging and condemnation and vilifying people. It's very challenging. It's very, very challenging.

JED: After almost 25 years in traditional corporate environment, in a very conservative, high-stress medical environment selling high-end medical devices, what you just said is very, very real.

It's extremely egocentric and, unfortunately, when you see something and you try and share from your soul, from your heart, from your spirit that, "Hey, you know what, this is what I see. This is what I feel because I'm in the trench, I see it," basically, you're ostracized because of your belief, because of your attitude, because you spoke up.

Awesome. Great, great, great!

Let me ask you another question. You know when you're having a conversation with someone, let's say you're sitting in the boardroom and you're talking with your clients, what is it that cues you into knowing that they're actually tracking and following your conversation or the communication that you're having with them? How are you aware that they're really acknowledging the fact

Why Can't We Say What We Mean?

that they hear you and they understand what you're saying?

FRAN: It's an interesting thing. You see the physiology change with people. It really is. As much as it's over-used, the light really comes on and you can see it in their eyes, even when what they are acknowledging makes them uncomfortable.

And I've had to practice this, of course, as this is my business, my job, my craft, is to tuning into people's body languages, but more than their physical body language, their physiological body language, the things that happen. You can see them shifting. You can see them responding.

I'm not a consultant, I'm an insultant. I go into companies to really try to inspire and ignite certain things to come out of them that, quite frankly, they don't appreciate.

JED: Does that have to do with the sweat off their brow and the color of their skin, and how often they rotate from left to right in the chair?

FRAN: Yeah, or you can see like their eyes, it's like a window shade. The eye kind of closes a little bit and it opens. I share that with them. I say, "You know, I'll tell you. You're going to come in and out of this session with me," especially if I'm with them for like an eight-hour day. They get triggered and on and off and on and off.

I say, "Hang in there, because I'm going to say things that are going to trigger you."

One of the most important things that people have to realize to get to the next level in a relationship, and certainly with communication, is this notion that what I'm experiencing with you is not about you.

When I say things to you, Jed, that you don't like, that's not about me. It's hard for people because what they want to do is say, "Oh, I don't like Fran Harris. I didn't like that she asked us to do this. I thought that was silly."

And I say to them, "What is it about, what's going on that makes you uncomfortable?"

"Oh, I'm not uncomfortable."

"Really, you're not uncomfortable? Really, you're not uncomfortable?"

Why Can't We Say What We Mean?

"No."

"What is it about what we just did that's making you have this opinion of me?"

"I don't have an opinion of you."

It's like understanding that it's not about me is one of the hardest things for people to do. We all want to make it about somebody else.

You've been in a relationship, right? You do something that irritates me. Let's say we were together, Jed, and you leave the orange juice out. "Jed, I've told you that 20 times. Why do you leave the orange juice out?"

I want to make that about you. Well, maybe it's my need for order. Maybe it's my obsessive-compulsiveness. But instead, I make it about you. That's one of the hardest things to get people to change. It's profoundly difficult.

Like one of my clients right now, they're starting to turn that corner. Oh, the things that are happening in their company are just amazing, because all they wanted to do before

I got on the scene was to vilify the boss, or vilify this person, or make this about this person.

As a result, they were unproductive, completely underperforming, and just having a horrible time in their job. Everything that happened to them, good or bad, was about somebody else.

JED: And that leads me then to the next series of two questions. What do you do to move someone from this position of pain to this position of future pleasure? Obviously, you have a skill set that helps you move from point A to point B.

I jumped from question 2 to question 10, but that's okay because this is what it's all about. It's about dialogue and what best suits the particular situation.

This question is actually multi-fold, because it's different with every person that you speak with.

Can you just give our audience some insight as to what you do to make that transition?

FRAN: The most powerful tool of transformation, in my opinion, is

Why Can't We Say What We Mean?

walking the talk. I can't walk into a corporation, they brought me in as an expert and I'm teaching them all of these transformative tools and giving them new skill sets. And then I'm not actually embodying those skill sets, the thing that I really believe that sets me apart from some of the people that they've seen.

In the midst of something that's so difficult, and you know, this is really work, this is really difficult, I never take it personally when I'm walking them through things and working them through things, and they are literally acting out and projecting their anger, frustration, hurt onto me, the trainer, the educator.

In that moment, I literally model what they need to do. I don't take it personally. I ask them and I'm very open. I don't let them vilify me and I never let them off the hook.

As a result of that, I never get engaged with the unhealthy behavior. See, that's what happens a lot in relationships, whether it's in business or personal. It really does take two to tango. If you never engage and you're constantly reflecting back to people and asking them to be accountable and not taking it personally, it defuses every single unhealthy behavior they have. It completely disarms them.

When that's happening, it's rough and tough, even on my end. A few weeks ago, a client and I were having drinks after the session and they said, "You do know that we're drinking because of you."

Isn't that great?

"This whole happy hour thing is because of you. We're drinking profusely because of you!"

But the funny thing was that they said it. I said, "This is great!" And it really was. I saw so much movement.

And they go, "Yeah, it's because you're not on this side."

I said, "If you think for one moment that it's easy for me to be on my side, it's not." Hey, all the emotional stuff is happening and I see how hard it is for these very capable, intelligent people who care about what's happening to have to journey through this. It's hard for me to

Why Can't We Say What We Mean?

maintain this objectivity. It's hard for me not to let this bother me.

It's like a parent, honestly. I don't know if you have children, but you want to let them off the hook. You love them, but you can't. You know, if I let them off the hook in this instance, we missed the opportunity to turn the corner.

For me, it's about being fully engaged in the moment and honoring where they are, but most importantly, modeling the behavior that I'm teaching them to model in their own organization.

JED: Let's jump around a little bit, because you just said something that is really, really powerful. Actually, for every single person that I've interviewed for this project, they have all basically focused on the same process.

This is generally the last question, but you brought it up. What is it that you do for yourself? This is a real critical, critical point in the development of healthy relationships, is the relationship you have with yourself.

For example, and this isn't the last question, but this is the last question that I normally ask.

As a teacher, trainer, mentor, human change agent, the power and influence that you have on those of us that you work with is very, very draining, it's very intense. What is it that you do to keep yourself healthy, keep yourself jazzed, keep yourself coming back every morning, keep your vision, your direction, your hunger, and your desire?

FRAN: Jazzed is a great word. I'm so utterly and completely ignited by change. When I see it, when I see people on the cusp of it, when I see they're about to turn the corner on something, when I see a light come on, I get so excited. That's why it's not draining to me. That's why at the end of that day I was like, "This was so much fun."

I see that happening in a room. I'm working with a room of 12 executives, and as hard as it's been for them, and I know it's been hard for them, they got through to a different place.

I never worked with anybody one-on-one, or even in groups, where

Why Can't We Say What We Mean?

they walked into the room in one place and then walk out in another place, even if it was just a centimeter.

That's the nature of this work. For me it's like, "Yes!"

It's probably because I'm an athlete. Every day you go and you know there's something that you can do better. Even if you shot 1% better from the free-throw line, that's the stuff that drives you and keeps you coming back and knowing that, "Tomorrow, I can shoot from the free-throw line."

For me, it's really about the potential that we, as humans, have as spiritual beings. We have just such incredible potential. When I'm working with people and I see them being so willing to be transformed, and not just change, but to literally do things and think about things in a completely different way, it completely excites me.

JED: That's the power of what you just said; the fact that you're focused on them. You're not focused on yourself. You're not focused on what it is that you do for them, but what actually they are doing for themselves. You're the catalyst in that room.

When you said that, I had this vision that they walk in with these chins down to the ground, and they have this drab look on their face. "I have to go through this all over again. What is this sensitivity stuff that I'm dealing with? I can't believe it."

The next thing you know they're walking out arm-in-arm with Dr. Harris, with grins on their faces going, "I can't believe she moved us from here to there."

FRAN: That's exactly it. It's so funny. The person that hired me for her team said, "We now have a year-long contract. The next thing we're doing," she said, "well, I want them to leave there feeling really good."

I know she said that because of how hard this work is. I said, "Well, you know we can't control that."

She goes, "I know, but I would just like them to feel really good."
And I said, "It's hard work."

It's really about perspective and how you view the work. I never loved

Why Can't We Say What We Mean?

practice, let me be very honest. There were days I enjoyed it more and there were instances where I loved it. But for the most part, it was not an enjoyable physical experience for most of us.

However, what you knew is that it's getting you to the next place, so you brought the best attitude you could. You had fun. You found things that you could really revel in, and that's what I try to get my clients to do.

I said, "Yes, this is going to be hard. You're going to be sweating. You're going to be feeling like you want to give up, but at the end of it.... We do it every day. We know how we're going to feel when we hit the showers. We're going to feel great. If you can just kind of keep that visual, then the next six hours with me or the next three days with me, we'll have our moments, our hills and valleys, but you already know how you're going to feel when the last buzzer sounds."

JED: I want to tell you, and everybody listening to this buzzer sound, it's currently 9 o'clock on the West Coast, and where Dr. Harris is right now it's 11 o'clock, and she's still got the kind of energy to step up to the plate.

That tells you a lot about her character and her personality and who she is. That's pretty impressive to me.

I do have to say that right now. It's been a long day and I thank you for your time.

Let me ask you this. Are there some tidbits that you can share and also a little bit about the services that you provide, your website, and so forth? Are there some tidbits that you can give our audience about what they may be able to do to improve their current situation, or resources that they can go to?

FRAN: I think every day, for me, it's about waking up with a new sense of possibility. Even when things haven't necessarily been orchestrated the way I want them, even though there are things that happen during the course of the day that I would have liked to have gone differently, I'm always reminding myself, and I do mean this literally, out loud, I'm reminding myself that I'm choosing my experience.

Why Can't We Say What We Mean?

That sounds simple, but sometimes I think a lot of people think that their experiences are happening to them. Like something happened today and I said, "Why are you choosing this experience when there are so many others that you enjoy? Why are you choosing this experience?"

In that instant, I was out of that experience. That's the main tidbit. I don't want to overload them with stuff. Just focus on that. Know that every single second of your day, of your life, you are choosing that experience.

If somebody cut you off, you chose that experience. Is somebody is passive-aggressive and you respond to it, you're choosing that experience.

I wake up every morning with $100 of emotional currency and I get to choose how I spend that currency. I'm not going to spend it being mad at you, Jed. I don't care what you do.

I'm not going to spend it being upset with the person who didn't pay their bills on time. I'm not going to spend it with the client that never can seem to make their payment on time, none of that. I just move right on through it.

I have $100 of emotional currency every single day.

JED: I love that analogy. That's great!

FRAN: It's going to be joyful spending for me.

JED: Yes. That's a vision that is regardless of wherever we are, whoever we are, wherever we get up, you start your day with a vision. You just gave me a brilliant vision. Every morning I get up, I put both feet on the floor and I do a 10/10, ten things I'm grateful for and 10 things that I'm going to attract into my life today.

It really is quite powerful when we do just that.

Dr. Harris, I have to say I am truly blessed to have had the opportunity to speak with you and interview you.

You can find Dr. Harris at www.franharris.com. Are there some other sites where they can find you?

FRAN: That's the main one, and www.franharris.com is a great one to start with because everything kind of

Why Can't We Say What We Mean?

	emanates from there. I'm going to be doing some really powerful programs and seminars over the second-half of the year, everything from a live broadcast online teaching people how to make six or seven figures as a speaker.
	If you go to www.franharris.com and opt in and get that free MP3 from me, you'll get notification of all that great stuff.
JED:	Isn't that awesome? I have to say I was in Dallas last week and I'm sorry that we didn't connect before that, because it would have been great to have met you. We will connect. We are definitely destined to connect with one another.
	I truly, truly appreciate the time that you've given and I look forward to many future conversations.
	Dr. Harris, thank you very, very much.
FRAN:	Thank you, Jed, my pleasure.

CHAPTER 7:
INTERVIEW WITH
DR. STAN HARRIS

Dr. Stan Harris

Dr. Stan "Breakthrough" Harris is perhaps the most entertaining, enlightening, and electrifying speaker on the circuit today. At age six he was jumped, beaten, tarred and feathered by a teenage gang. He started in Martial Arts (Isshin-Ryu Karate) to learn how to protect himself, and now 38 years later is one of few who has attained the highest honors of **10th Degree Black Belt**. He's been inducted into the **Black Belt Hall of Fame**, as well as the **Motivational Speakers Hall of Fame** with Get Motivation.com.

He has driven over two million miles using a combination of martial art skills and his energetic

Why Can't We Say What We Mean?

speaking ability to move crowds as large as 17,000, speaking in all 50 states and 27 countries.

He's been a college professor with a Doctorate in Divinity, a successful network marketer, a life and business trainer/coach. He's been to the top of four companies and recently built an organization from 0 to 22,000 distributors in only five short months, earning over $250,000.00. He is co-author of *Walking with the Wise Entrepreneur* along with Donald Trump, Les Brown, T. Harv Eker, Zig Ziglar, Dan Kennedy, and many others. "Dr. Breakthrough" believes you may be one step from your next breakthrough.

Contact Dr. Stan at www.DrBreakThrough.com and get the same effective tools and resources for your success.

INTERVIEW

JED: Good morning, everyone. This is Jed Reay, "The Communicator." It is my privilege to introduce to you "Dr. Breakthrough," Dr. Stan Harris. Dr. Harris is going to discuss with us and talk to us about communication.

What I want to start off with, which I think is just fascinating about this whole relationship and how I came to know Dr. Harris, "Dr. Breakthrough," is through a connection and what communication is all about. That's what we're doing. That's why all of us are connected.

Until we make a connection with someone and find out what it is that we either have or don't have in common with them, and how we help one another to grow in our life, we cannot develop and grow fascinating relationships.

This book that I'm compiling was at the suggestion of Stephen Pierce and Alicia Pierce, and they introduced me to "Dr. Breakthrough." What I find so fascinating about Stan Harris is that he also made some major connections in the area of communication with very powerful people, specifically women.

In my case, this project didn't have a whole lot of powerful women, so it was really, really interesting when Dr. Harris and I decided to have a conversation. He asked me some very key questions, and lo and behold, it opened the world up to me.

So without further ado, Dr. Harris, welcome to the call.

STAN: Well, thank you. It's a privilege and a pleasure, a treat and a treasure, a

Why Can't We Say What We Mean?

joy beyond measure to be on the phone with you and be a part of this powerful series.

JED: Thank you very much. Let me start off by asking you just a little bit about your background, just a brief few minutes here about who you are and what you bring to the table to help people make connections, communicate with the world, and grow as a human being.

STAN: Sure, I'll tell you my background. As a 6-year-old boy, I got jumped by a gang of teenagers. They started clubbing me. They threw me out in the middle of a field and left me there.

I grew up in a single parent home in the ghettos, obviously a real rough section of town. That was something that dramatically affected my life. I tell people, "Within your pain is hidden power."

Somebody very aptly said, "Trouble never comes to a woman or a man unless she brings a nugget of good in her hand." When the trouble comes, people sometimes concentrate on the trouble and not the good that comes along with it.

The good that came with that was I was motivated to learn how to protect myself, and I got started in martial arts. That was 38 years ago. Now I find myself as a 10the Degree Black Belt, less than 100 in the world of six billion people, voted to the Black Belt Hall of Fame, as well as the Motivational Speakers Hall of Fame.

A lot of that was because of what I went through as a child, and so forth, and so it's just been a great life. I've been in all 50 states and 21 countries, traveling and communicating and speaking with people. It's a whole fascination with people. We're all intricate beings, and it's a wonderful thing how God made us, and how when we relate to each other we can learn from each other.

That's one of the things they taught me in martial arts that I think enabled my communication skills, and that is simply this. Everybody knows something that I don't know. Hence, I must probe and find out what it is. Thus, all men, women, and children are my teachers.

When you have that type of attitude, you're always in the probing mode.

Why Can't We Say What We Mean?

	I'm not out there trying to have to prove something to somebody. I'm actually trying to extract information.
JED:	Sure. I appreciate this, because this just reinforces in me and this project, this book, of how important it is to have people like you contribute and help people, guide people and direct people. Let's get right to it.
STAN:	Sure.
JED:	First question, what is the biggest barrier that people need to break through in order to communicate more effectively?
STAN:	You said the key word, "breakthrough."
JED:	Amen.
STAN:	First of all, I'm the world's only breakthrough speaker. Perhaps I ought to clarify that and go right into that. People always say, "What is the difference between a breakthrough speaker and the motivational speaker? I thought you were just a motivational speaker."

I'm actually beyond motivation to a breakthrough, and here's what I mean by that. Motivation is good. It's kind of like taking a shower. You just need one every day, kind of like the motivational speaker gets the caterpillar to move a little faster.

But as a breakthrough speaker, I assist the caterpillar into getting into the cocoon, and then out of the cocoon as a beautiful butterfly. That's a total transformation.

In order for us really to communicate better, we really have to have a total transformation in the way we've been doing things, the way we've been thinking.

I would say the biggest barrier, which by the way, I teach people in my travels that barriers were not made to hinder us. Barriers were made to be broken. That's the great thing about it. When I learned the concept that barriers were made to be broken, not only is it possible to break these barriers, but that's the reason why they're there.

JED: Yes, yes.

STAN: That's breakthrough explained. I want to say this. This is pretty

Why Can't We Say What We Mean?

	strong, but I think the biggest barrier that hinders people from communication is called "prejudice."
JED:	Interesting.
STAN:	In Latin prejudice, "prae" means before and "judicium" means judge or come to a conclusion. Literally, the word prejudice means come to a conclusion before the facts are in.
	Again, we're particularly talking about business relationships here, but how many times do you and I come to a conclusion before we have all of the facts in, and we try to communicate or talk to somebody based on what we think that we really don't even know? I know I've done this in the past many, many times, and that's why I had to learn to break through this barrier.
JED:	Isn't that true.
STAN:	In fact, when many people are talking, Jed, I would oftentimes come to a conclusion about what I was going to answer before they even finished. Here's part of the reason why.

The average person has a speaking ability of about 200 to 250 words per minute. We can listen at about 450 words per minute. The tendency is that we can finish the statement in our mind, think about it, and then come back.

But sometimes the person is still talking and they do a little change on us, so when we come back, all of a sudden we get two pieces of information that don't quite fit.

The pre-judging, or coming to a conclusion before the facts are in, that's something that I believe is the biggest barrier that will hinder communication.

We can break through it, and we should break through it. I believe what you're doing is going to be part of the thing that is going to help some people to be alerted to it, to be aware of it, and to be able to break through it.

JED: Amen. Thank you very much. That is very, very true. That whole notion of what you just said is the basis for misunderstanding, the basis for poor communication between two people. That was perfect. Thank you very, very much.

Why Can't We Say What We Mean?

That being said, you have the ability to connect and communicate with a lot of people at different levels. Why is that possible?

STAN: I learned a long time ago that people listen to their favorite radio station, and it's called "WIIFM." I'll say it again, "WIIFM," which stands for "What's in it for me."

What I found out a long time ago is that if I'm going to be able to effectively communicate with people and connect with people, then I don't want to pre-judge or come to a conclusion before the facts are in.

This is one of the reasons, also, why it's very hard for people in business and sales, why they have such a hard time. Before they ever talk to the person, before they ever do anything, they have their mind already figured out what they think that person needs and what that person ought to buy. We don't want to do that.

The reason I've been able to communicate and connect is simply this. When you understand what a person's favorite station is, what's in it for them, now you come from a

www.jedthecommunicator.com

standpoint of offering them what they want, need or desire.

The question is, "How can I offer someone what they need, what they want, and what they desire if I don't know what it is?"

I have to be able to effectively communicate and find out what they're interested in, find out what they like, find out what they want.

I once was part of a network marketing company, and the CEO had written a book called *Guaranteed Prospects*. He and I were doing a meeting together. We flew in on the private corporate jet. He mentioned to the crowd, "You know, Dr. Stan Harris is the only person that I know that doesn't need to read my book. This guy can recruit people at-will. Literally, he could sell ice to an Eskimo."

I got up to speak afterwards and I said, "I appreciate your comments you meant as a compliment, and I thank you so much for that, but technically, Eskimos don't need ice."

I can't recruit people at-will, but here's what I do. I find out what people are interested in. I find out

Why Can't We Say What We Mean?

what people like. I find out what people need, and I simply connect them to the person or to that thing that helps and assists them in getting what they want.

I tell people, literally, "It's a real easy deal when you come that way. It's not a struggle. It's not all the hard work. It's called 'working smart.'"

JED: Yes, wonderful. Thank you.

STAN: Sure

JED: Some people are natural communicators, others are not. What keys can you give us that would allow the average person to open up the doors of communication?

STAN: That's an excellent question. We've talked a little bit about that already, but I guess to put it in a form, again, if you think about a door that would hinder or block communication, if you want to get through that door, it's one thing to break the door down, but why don't we just put the key in it to open that door? Listening would be one of the keys that open the door.

I would like to say nonjudgmental listening. One of the problems with communication is sometimes, some of us have gotten to a place where we learn to listen, but we're listening for specific things. We're looking for specific things and we start jumping and grabbing those things, and then forming things based on what we heard. Technically, most people hear what they really want to hear.

If you look for something long enough, you'll tend to find it. I call it "non-judgmental listening," just learning to listen. Let that person just pull out.

I found that people are so hurting today and so hungry to find someone who would truly listen to them, listen to them in a nonjudgmental way, that when they finally find that person, they open up. Obviously, when they open up, you and I have an opportunity now to find out what they are really all about.

I would also say to notice the average conversation. Oftentimes another person will butt in before the other person is done. Or after they listen and the second person starts talking, the first person says, "Wait a minute. No, that's not really what I

Why Can't We Say What We Mean?

meant, that's not really what I'm talking about."

One would be listening and the other one, I would say, would be learning. Be in a state of learning. Again, when you understand the fact that everybody knows something that I don't know, we must find out what it is and learn it for ourselves.

If you're always in a mode of learning, people love to feel like they are teaching somebody something. I love to learn. The more I know, the better it makes me.

When I taught martial arts I used to tell the guys, "If I'm ever going to teach you anything, I first of all have to break your nose."

They were like, "Break my nose?"

"No, not your N O S E, but your K N O W S. In other words, I can't teach you anything if you think you know it all. You have to first break your KNOWS."

I'm constantly like a sponge trying to learn things. I've found out that when people pick up that you're willing to learn, that you don't have the "I know all attitude," people have a tendency to open up and feel like they are connected.

Many times when I deal with people, they say this to me, "I feel like I've known you all my life. I feel like we've known each other for a long time." I take that as a compliment.

The last thing that I would say is love. Love yourself, and then you'll have enough love for this individual. When you love someone, you do what's best.

Love's not necessarily an emotion. Love is a commitment to goodwill. When you have these keys and you're willing to listen and learn and love, I'm telling you the doors of communication will swing wide open and your ability to connect with people will be awesome!

JED: All right! That's awesome. Thank you. That being said, who do you attribute your success to? Who and what influenced your communication skills in this positive way?

STAN: Several things, first of all, my mother obviously. I grew up in a single parent home. Mom didn't believe in welfare, she worked two jobs to take

Why Can't We Say What We Mean?

care of us, so I didn't know what this welfare thing was. I figured if it's so bad that you've got to work two jobs, you've got to work two jobs. My mom didn't communicate a whole lot by what she said, but more by what she did.

Just by watching her, that was a big thing. As I grew older, I got some different mentors and different people. Somebody gave me a book called *The Greatest Salesman In The World*, by Og Mandino. One statement he made in there is that when you meet a person, and you don't even verbally say it but just to yourself, you say, "I meet you with love in my heart." That one statement was incredible.

I was a person who grew up not loving myself, because of all the rejection I faced. I grew up in a single parent home. My dad left when I was three, and growing up where I grew up, I was in this arena trying to prove myself.

All of a sudden, one day it dawned on me I didn't have to prove myself. I just needed to improve myself. When you're trying to prove yourself, you can't really communicate with people.

"Oh, my goodness, you're always messed, you're always intimidated and are intimidating people." But when you're just improving yourself, that's a different thing.

Reading this book by Og Mandino really helped me.

I also read *The Five Love Languages*, by author Dr. Gary Chapman at www.fivelovelanguages.com. This book wasn't about business, but you know what I found out? When I read that book and started implementing it into my relationships, it also enhanced my business.

Very briefly, he talked about if you make a deposit in a person's emotional love bank, then that's helping them. When you make a withdrawal, you have more withdrawals than deposits.

He was saying, for instance, if I spoke Spanish and you spoke English, I could say to you in Spanish, "You're a wonderful person. You're doing a great thing." But you really wouldn't understand

Why Can't We Say What We Mean?

what I'm saying, because I'm not speaking your language.

Gary boiled it down to this. For some people, it's words of affirmation, the way they describe love or the way they receive love, or pick up or emotionally feel or sense love. With communication, it's more than what you hear. It's what you sense, it's words of affirmation.

These people need a verbal pat on the back. That's big, especially if you're in network marketing or some type of business where you're dealing with people. People are hurting so much. They hear those words of affirmation, for somebody to praise them and lift them up.

By the way, I tell people, you're either going to live up to your compliments or down to your criticisms."

If you're a person who wants to have influence, learn to find the good in someone, and then brag on it. You will, literally, help to bring that out.

JED: Amen

STAN: With some people it's words, and with some people it's quality time.

JED: Right.

STAN: These are the people that words are important to them, but it doesn't mean the same to them as you actually spending quality time talking to them, or quality time looking them in the eyes, or whatever the case may be.

The third one is acts of service. That's doing things out of the ordinary, not every day, but the little, special, out-of-the-ordinary things that tell that person, "You're special to me."

For some, it's gift-giving and receiving, and they like to receive gifts or give gifts. It doesn't have to be purchased. It can just be something that you made.

The last thing is physical touch and closeness. It's amazing for a person to be physically touched and close. It doesn't take a whole lot to discern that, because this is the person that when they talk to you, they're very close to you, or they're always touching you.

Why Can't We Say What We Mean?

A person who is physical touch and closeness, and you're a person who's gift-giving and receiving and you want to express your care and concern to them by giving them a gift, and they're physical touch and closeness, you're kind of missing the boat a little bit.

It kind of helped me zero in on some factors. In fact, I started using that with my children, and then I started using it with my business. I found a secret, and that is this. People like to do business with people that they like. And get this, people like to do business.

This isn't good English, but it's a good message. People like to do business with people that they like, and people like to do business with people they feel liked by.

JED: That's true.

STAN: In other words, people that they feel like them.

JED: That's right.

STAN: When you can speak a person's emotional love language, or when you understand the person, they get this sense that this person really cares. Bill Bailey, he's a guy, oh my goodness, he influenced Les Brown years ago. Actually, Jim Rohn worked for him for seven years.

Bill Bailey built a business grossing $64 million a month back in the 70s with no fax machine, no anything. I think this is one of the things we're talking about with communication. Now we live in a day where it's high-tech and literally low-touch.

What we really want is high-tech, high-touch, to be able to communicate and be effective. He said, "Young Dr. Stan, we had to train and learn people. Rather, help them to learn the ability to communicate and work with others."

I asked him this question, I said, "Mr. Bailey, what in the world did you do to create $64 million a month in income?"

He said, "Young Dr. Stan, that's the wrong question."

I said, "Okay, sir. What's the right question?"

He said, "The question you should have asked me is, 'What did I do to

Why Can't We Say What We Mean?

create value in the lives of people that resulted in $64 million a month?'"

I found out it was all about touching and communicating with people.

Mr. Bailey taught me this. Oftentimes, when I talk to people I'll say, "Jed, do you mind if I ask you a question?"

It sounds so simple, but people think, "Wow! This guy is nice. He's asking me if."

I'll say, "Do you mind if I say something?" or, "Do you mind if I ask you this?" and that tends to help people to open up a little bit.

Sometimes, of course, there are different things that people have used, but these are the people and things that have influenced my life the most. I know that was a little long. I'm sorry, but that's it.

JED: No, no. This is wonderful. The whole point of this book, the whole point of our lives, you and I coming together and making a connection is to broaden both of our horizons, broaden the opportunity that we bring to our audience and to everybody that we touch.

Every life that we come in contact with benefits all those others that we come in contact with. I am truly blessed, Dr. Stan, very, very much.

Let me ask you another question. The whole idea of advanced communication, you have this ability to communicate far, far above what a lot of people would say is normal communication. I would beg to differ. I would say communication is something that's learned, and that all you've got to do is practice.

That being said, what would you suggest to do to improve in this area of consciousness? Let me ask you this. Your company, your services, who you are, what can you do to help our audience?

STAN: Obviously, my website is www.drbreakthrough.com and my whole thrust is helping people to break through barriers that would hinder them, whether it's in the financial arena, the spiritual arena, or relationships.

I have a special CD that I train on how to talk your way to the top,

Why Can't We Say What We Mean?

which talks a lot about communication. I also have some information and things on communication itself. I'm avid and I'm so passionate about growing as a person and reading whatever you can read, listening to whatever you can listen to, to help you to improve.

The essence of this, and for all of us, is these types of situations where we meet someone and it's like, "My goodness, we have so much in common," or, "Oh, my goodness, I just felt like I've known you all my life!" And you meet other people you don't have that same feeling with.

Part of that is because you're connecting on a deeper spiritual level, you're connecting on who you are as a person. I think it was George Washington that said, "Empty your wallet into your mind and your mind will fill your wallet."

People that get into business think they can make more money by working the business more. No. You make more money by improving as a person more. Improving as a person more is being able to communicate more.

Copyright © 2008. Jed A. Reay. All rights reserved.

Since we live here on earth with other people, we need to learn to connect with those people. That's one of the things I do also with some coaching programs that I have.

I just want to say again, I just appreciate you and what you're doing, because this is something that's definitely necessary and needed. Unless somebody helps us to become aware of some things, we don't even know what's happening. We are sincere people, but sometimes we are sincerely wrong. We just need to make the necessary adjustments.

JED: I thank you for that. This leads me to bring us to our last question. Ultimately, this has been a lifelong passion for me to talk about how we communicate and some of the difficulties that we have, especially in this day and age, and the energies it requires, the amount of time in a day.

Everybody has the same 24 hours. With some people, it's quite amazing how they can focus their energies and be so deeply engrained in what it is that they're doing to try to help other people.

Why Can't We Say What We Mean?

It took a couple of my mentors and mastermind group to point me in the right direction, and blessed, here I am. Thank you.

As a teacher, as a trainer, mentor, as a human change agent, you have a powerful, powerful influence on us. When we come in contact with you, or come in contact with anybody which you direct us to or associate us with, what do you do to maintain your vision, direction, your thirst, your hunger and your desire to continue? It has to be exhausting.

STAN: That's a very good and excellent question. Oftentimes I ask people this question, especially leaders, because I do a lot of training leaders. "Do you know what it is that fills your tank and fires you up?"

There was a guy, a preacher, of years gone by named John Wesley, and he preached in the Established Church of England. It is said this preacher was too hot and they kicked him out. He went across the street and he would speak from his father's tombstone.

They said they had more people that would come hear him out at his father's tombstone in the elements than would go to the nice, comfortable church.

Somebody said, "John Wesley, why is it so many people come to hear you preach?"

He said simply, "I just put myself on fire and people come watch me burn."

I try to get people to understand that if you can find out what puts you on fire, what stimulates you, what keeps your tank full, then you can always be a person of influence and you don't have to go through what I call the "burn-out," which a lot of people end up going through.

I have something that I wrote years ago that I read to myself, because I figured out what fires me up. I fill my tank up on purpose all of the time. When you get in at night, you take your cell phone and you put it on a charger. If you're a person like I am, you also put it in your car. We each have to have those things that charge us up. This is something that I read, and if you don't mind I would like to read it real quick to the listeners.

Why Can't We Say What We Mean?

JED: Please, please.

STAN: This is literally what I go through in the morning and helps me, and sometimes I do this at night as well. It's something I wrote at 4:30 in the morning. I was speaking at a convention with a bunch of other powerful speakers and this came to me. I just started jotting the words down.

> Wow! What a great day to be alive. I feel dynamite. I like me. I accept me. I love me. I'm going to have a super fantastic day today, because I'm too blessed to be depressed. I'm too blessed to be stressed. I'm too glad to be sad, and I'm too anointed to be disappointed.
>
> Circumstances are lining themselves in my favor. I am healthy, physically fit, and intellectually equipped. I have wisdom far beyond my years. I am an extraordinary person with incredible abilities, which I will use to add value to other people's lives, because I know that as I help others reach their

dreams, I will automatically reach my own.

I anticipate meeting the person or group of people today who are willing to use their power, wealth, and influence to help me achieve my dreams. All day long people will go out of their way to bless me. Today, I will add great value to someone's life. I will show compassion to those in need. I will give strength to the weak and inspiration to the weary. Someone needs what I have to offer and I gladly make myself available.

I embrace abundance and it embraces me. I am abundant in every good way. I am an abundance magnet. I like money and it likes me, and it is attracted to me, and it comes abundantly from many sources. I use my money wisely, because it is a tool to use to help those in need.

I am experiencing great victories, supernatural turnarounds, and miraculous breakthroughs in the midst of

Why Can't We Say What We Mean?

great impossibilities. I am an over-comer. If my mountain cannot be removed, I will develop and practice my mountain climbing skills.

I was broke, busted, and disgusted, but now I'm rich, growing, and overflowing. I may experience a setback, but setbacks are only setups for comebacks. Setbacks pave the way for comebacks. I make lemonade out of life's lemons. And if life knocks me down, I will fall on my back realizing as long as I can look up, I can get up.

I commit to pain for my dreams with preparation, so that I won't have to live with my nightmares of regret. I do not procrastinate, because procrastination leads to devastation. It is the assassination of my destination, thus I will act now! I am a doer. I get results that last.

I now release the champion that is inside of me. I am the leader that multitudes of people are looking for. I choose to succeed today and every day hereafter.

Watch out world, here I come!

JED: Oh, "Dr. Breakthrough," that was awesome! Thank you very, very, very much. That was a wonderful way to conclude this.

I can't begin to thank you for your contribution to the human race, your contribution to us as followers, listeners, viewers, and those of us that really, truly want to break through and break those chains and learn to change from where we are to where we want to go.

Dr. Stan Harris, I thank you so very much. All of us are very blessed because we know you now.

STAN: I thank you also, and I look forward to hearing from some of the people who will read this or hear this. I just encourage them in some way, because my whole life is dedicated to assisting other people to breaking through to the success that they desire and that they deserve.

Why Can't We Say What We Mean?

JED: Thank you. We'll conclude this interview and we'll move on to the next one. This is Jed Reay, "The Communicator" and "Dr. Breakthrough" signing off.

Copyright © 2008. Jed A. Reay. All rights reserved.

CHAPTER 8:
INTERVIEW WITH
ARTEMIS LIMPERT

Ms. Artemis Limpert

Artemis Limpert is a personal coach, speaker, and master in creating successful teamwork. She has been through great struggles of self-doubt, of facing her own shortcomings and the myriad ways in which they hobbled relationships with others.

Artemis is an **EAS Body-for-Life © Grand Champion for 2000** and a current spokesperson for Anthony Robbins' latest infomercial "Get the Edge." In her network marketing business, she shares her highly effective coaching and teaching methods that changed her business from "No Profit" to being at the top her company within 24 months.

Artemis has unimpeachable integrity, unlimited energy, dedication to the development of others, and the unique

Why Can't We Say What We Mean?

ability to cut to the heart of the matter with such humor, wit and wisdom that she easily disarms her audiences, allowing them to achieve the real breakthroughs they desire to move forward in their personal lives and their business enterprises.

Artemis is available for **personal coaching and speaking** and can be reached directly at 1-800-423-5715 or www.paidmydues.net.

INTERVIEW

JED: Hello, this is Jed Reay. We just completed a three-day leadership emersion, and Artemis has given me the pleasure, and I have the pleasure, of being here in her home to interview her for a book that I'm writing.

I would just like to say thank you very much, Artemis. That was a wonderful three-day event and I look forward to a much longer and developed relationship with you. I appreciate that very much.

ARTEMIS: Oh, it was fun. One of the things that's been fun is that Jed and I have had a chance to know each other for at least three years. Has it been three or four, somewhere in there?

JED: About three years.

ARTEMIS: The fun of that is seeing where the different developments of communication of skill sets and of business go, and to be able to come back and forth with each other. I actually see a lot of strength in new things that you and I can see together that we didn't see before. That's really fun.

JED: That was the whole premise for doing this interview. I have a communication background, and I really, truly am passionate about being able to communicate with someone. With the advent of the Internet and emails and all this fancy technology, we tend to lose the human aspect of our communication. That's kind of what I would like to talk to you about today, ask you a few questions, and get your input on the human element of communication.

This book is looking at the dichotomy between a normal human relationship that we have, and the way we communicate with one another, the whole notion that here we have this medium which is supposed to improve our communications. We can interact

Why Can't We Say What We Mean?

with people in moments over hundreds of thousands of miles away, but is the quality of that communication good?

I would start off by asking you, what is it about human communication that you think is important, and what is it that we need to look at, or we need to analyze or need to study, need to think about when we're communicating with one another in a business arena?

ARTEMIS: Let me help your audience with just a little bit of my background, as to where some of these insights came from. First of all, my background started off as a hairdresser. I went back to college in my twenties and studied business. Then I moved to Washington DC and started working for nonprofits and worked in the sales arena.

I then went to work for for-profits and worked in the sales arena again. I then decided to get into real-profit, as you're doing and as you're helping others now by showing them how to do that.

The skills at each of those levels were completely different. The most important skills that I've had to learn were when I moved into real-profit, which is becoming an entrepreneur, deciding how to communicate from the essence of who I was, rather than from the essence of through something else.

What I'll say got confronted for me, because I thought moving into my own business, especially the sales background, I thought basically that it would be fairly easy to be honest. I thought that I would learn a few things from the industries, but I didn't think it would be hard. And yet, it was tremendously frightening.

It took me a good 18 months to relax into myself. I kept asking myself in that first year, "Why is this so different?" I realized that I had the luxury in my own business to spend a lot of time doubting myself, where in regular business I knew I would get fired.

JED: Right

ARTEMIS: The change of knowing how to talk, or just because you had friends of family, or even because you've been in business doesn't mean that you really understand the styles of communication or how to use

Why Can't We Say What We Mean?

influence, or how to even relax into who you are to speak from a genuine place. That is actually what opens everything.

JED: Let me ask you about that. When we look at the way that we have an interaction, face to face, what is it that you think is important to be able to take away from or provide to the interaction? For example, I personally believe from my perspective that I have to give before I get in a conversation.

ARTEMIS: Right, right.

JED: I need to fully understand what this other person's needs are before my needs are fulfilled.

ARTEMIS: Right, right.

JED: Maybe you can enlighten me and my audience a little bit on your perspective, on the characteristics of that, how you know the feeling for that. Plain and simple, some of these people may not have a strong communication background.

ARTEMIS: That's true, that's true. A lot of reciprocity that Jed just talked about is very key. It's very fascinating that

Copyright © 2008. Jed A. Reay. All rights reserved.

you begin to understand that there are a few techniques.

The other thing that I will share is that I was used to face-to-face communications. Face-to-face communications are different, and it's somewhat easier because there are a lot of cues that you get. You get someone's facial expressions, you get their voice, and you get their body language. There's a whole bunch of stuff.

You'll find that when many of us go to the phone or go to the Internet, we can be a little bit clumsy, because we don't get those cues. Every different style of communication I've found is slightly different.

When I went on the phone, it was harder for me. I didn't have all the clues that I was used to. Therefore, I got a little more sterile and a little bit more formal. Of course, that doesn't make the same interactions.

When I started to teach on conference call lines, which are muted, that's a whole other style. I thought, "Okay, this is still on the phone, that's a different style." Speaking to a group on a muted call where you have to be able to draw

Why Can't We Say What We Mean?

out of yourself a different level of energy was another style.

The Internet is a whole other style, once again. Webinars require something different. If you and I have an assumption that all of these should be equal, and just because I've had good friends and talked on the phone this should be easy, you're going to be too hard on yourself. You're probably going to eliminate yourself from the game of free enterprise way too fast.

The appreciation is that each median has is its style.

I think one of the biggest things for those that are working over the Internet is that for many people who are shyer, quieter, and want to work on the Internet to make a lot of money, they assume that, "I don't have to deal with this communication thing."

JED: Correct.

ARTEMIS: I see that you're already smiling, because those of us that have worked on the Internet realize that for many people who are working on the Internet, communication is still key.

Copyright © 2008. Jed A. Reay. All rights reserved.

Understanding human nature when you're doing it through the written word, or you're doing it through video, or you're doing it in person, basically, there are principles. The development of skill isn't something you can get away from, no matter what you try to do.

JED: I agree. I don't think that really there is any skill difference between those two if you're going to be successful.

ARTEMIS: Right

JED: The whole notion, and that's what actually prompted all of this, is that we can literally go into business. The growth of the home-based business marketplace, the small business marketplace internationally has exploded. Within 15 minutes, if you know what you're doing, you can get a URL, you can get a website up, a Google account set up and have traffic to your website. If you don't know how to communicate to that population, to anybody for that matter, then you run the risk of, obviously, you're going to fail.

ARTEMIS: Yes

JED: There are no two ways around it. That's why we're having this conversion, for that dichotomy

Why Can't We Say What We Mean?

between what people really, truly believe that they can accomplish versus what's real.

ARTEMIS: That's it, that's it.

JED: The whole point of having interaction, of having valuable conversations with one person or a group of people is real critical. That's why we're here talking about this.

ARTEMIS: That's exactly right. A lot of the clients that hire me, their first thing that they share is, "If you're going through this, then this will be enlightening or helpful, or make you feel like you're normal?"

I say, "Doesn't that mean that we're a little bit crazy in our own way?"

A lot of them say, "You know, I used to be so good at whatever I was in my old world." Then they go to step out into this higher level, and their biggest frustration is, "Why is this so hard?"

What I would want to say to each of you is the first thing I try to say to people who are coaching with me, and that is it's not so important what you're good at now.

Those of you in network marketing, those of you that are coming in direct sales, and many of you might be doing some online marketing as well, it's not so much what you are coming with that's going to be the key thing right now. It's going to be what you're willing to learn.

Right now it's going to be key that you are really hungry to give yourself room to learn, and then to experiment without judgment.

JED: That means we weren't born with these skills?

ARTEMIS: You know, I wonder sometimes if we weren't born with them, and then it got knocked out of us and we're trying to re-put them in.

If you watch babies, if you watch little kids, they're very good at adjusting their style. In their own way, before they talk or even after they talk, they're very good at engaging others. Before they even talk they do certain things.

Have you ever seen little kids in a grocery store? They have ways of

Why Can't We Say What We Mean?

getting your attention, even at flirting. When kids are toddlers and talking, it's the way that they'll pout. It's very fascinating that they're experimenting with their power, and it works.

I think there are a whole bunch of things that you do, depending on how you're schooled and what your family rules are, and then different things that you might be good at. I always joke with Blair, who majored in physics. He says, "Yes, that's a very human thing." And now here he is in network marketing and direct sales.

I think a lot of times we develop where we're comfortable. Later on, the key thing is that you ask yourself, "Is what I'm comfortable with actually getting me where I want to be?"

I'm sure for many of you, the reason why you went into network marketing, went into direct sales, or even looking at online marketing is you might have developed your skills down the road, and now you're saying "This is not the profit life that I want," or "This is not the way that I want to make money."

If I had known in my twenties to ask myself not what I'm good at, but where can I develop where there are markets that are growing and where it's exciting, and what skills would I have to develop to be able to play in that game, I would have gone here first.

Instead, I developed my skills around what I'm good at. What I thought I was good at was very limited, versus what I could become good at. Those are completely different things. Even now, if you ask yourself, forget what you're good at. I still watch people say, "But that's not my personality, that's not where I'm comfortable."

That's again where I say, "It doesn't matter what you're good at right now, it matters what you're willing to become good at. It also matters that you honor why you're hungry to do whatever this new business venture is."

JED: Basically, what you're saying is that you can be taught.

ARTEMIS: I am saying that.

JED: We can teach these skills?

Why Can't We Say What We Mean?

ARTEMIS: I'm saying that one of the key things to be willing to be taught and being coachable is it's okay to not be comfortable.

We were talking about a young man who is 13 now, but he was 11 at the time when he was sharing this. One of the things that this young man said was that he took a course first on investing. It was a 5-day course.

He said that three of these days on the course of investing were teaching everyone, mostly adults that were in their 40s, 50s, and 60s, about investing. Most of these three days were teaching how to act, in spite of fear and greed, learning how to make decisions outside fear and greed, to where this young man practices every day how to engage in the market he's choosing to engage in.

In fact, he's engaging in markets to create residual income, both in network marketing, in real estate and in investing, and in other things as well.

He said, "One of the things I do is I practice making decisions outside of fear and outside of greed."

I hope that that is very enlightening, because I find that most adults that I try and coach are trying to get away from fear, rather than practice making decisions outside of it. "Yes, I feel the fear."

That's really cool, because that means every day in whatever median I'm trying to learn, the key thing is not to try and wait until fear goes away, but to say, "Hey, Jed, hey, Artemis. You know, I want to do this along side," or, "Can you give me the skill set? I'm going to take a deep breath and I'm going to practice it until such a time that becomes more natural to me."

The biggest thing that you've got to embrace, or you've got to let yourself do, is that you've got to be willing to realize that failing forward is a very powerful thing all of the time.

I often tell the story of Thomas Watson, when he spoke at Harvard or Yale. I'm forgetting which one it is, but a young man who was 19 came up to him and said, "What is the secret of your success?"

Why Can't We Say What We Mean?

Thomas Watson said to him, "Do you really want to know?" which I think is a hint right there.

Many people ask questions, and the key thing is, do you really want to know?

JED: They're really not interested in the answer.

ARTEMIS: The second thing that he said to this young man is, "If I tell you, will you commit to do it?" And that's another clue right there.
This young man said, "Yes."

Thomas Watson said, "Double your failure rate."

For every one of us, in developing our communication styles and in realizing it's more than just talking, I think you realize that the first time you go out to start communicating through your own businesses, you start realizing there is all kinds of stuff that pops up. You just keep realizing to double your failure rate.

JED: Let me ask you another question. With the massive growth we're having, and the borders seem not to be there anymore, we're growing internationally at a more drastic rate than ever before. Are there some cultural differences? Is there anything you do differently, say, in Australia or in England, anywhere outside of North America? Is there something that you would do differently?

ARTEMIS: That's a great question. One of the things that's interesting that I've discovered over the last eight years in working with people from all over is I used to think and feel a little bit intimidated.

One of the things that you and I want to know is that human beings are human beings, and we all really, basically, have very similar steps that we have to go through in developing ourselves.

I was recently in Singapore, and the cultural things that were different are you're not going to chew gum there, that's for sure. That's against the law. They have very severe punishment to make sure. They still cane over there.

JED: She's here, so she must not have been chewing any gum.

Why Can't We Say What We Mean?

ARTEMIS: That's it. I didn't even pack my gum there, just to make sure. There's caning that happens there if you chew your gum. Also, when someone hands you a business card, they hand it to you end to end, like this, for you to look at first. Then they hand it to you, and you don't put it in your pocket and you don't put it down on a table.

When you're handing things, that's the way you do it, to show it, and then you appreciate their style of things.

Can I tell you what happened at the end of the event? There were people who came out throughout the event and said, "Thank you. The stages you were sharing about entrepreneurship were so enlightening and so key."

One of the things that I train people is in educating their expectations, because that's key to embracing where you're going. At the end, there were all of these women that came up to me. They had the exact same question that American women had, that Australian women had, that women of New Zealand had, that women in England and in Europe had.

JED: Interesting.

ARTEMIS: "Can a mom really do a business and raise her family? Can it really happen, because there's always that pull between disappointing your family or disappointing your business."

JED: I'll be darned.

ARTEMIS: There are certain things that are very predictable, while there are slight cultural things. The key thing that's the same is human nature. The person that you and I have to get to know the best is ourselves.

Recognizing that for myself, I used to feel really pressured that there was something that I needed to do for you or for each person. When I got into network marketing, I used to be terrified of those 15 minutes before a meeting when I had to go down and mingle. I was terrible at small talk.

There was a woman who was so good at it, and it was so funny because I was thinking, "Oh, I've got to hold on to what she does and what she says."

Why Can't We Say What We Mean?

After a couple of weeks, I was watching her and I was realizing, "You know what, all she does is really have a sincere interest in them."

What do you do? What are you loving right now about what you are doing? What are the stressful points about what you're doing? What are some of the dreams you have about what you would like to add to your life or your income right now?"

After a couple of weeks I was saying, "I can't believe after four years this has completely stressed me out. I was thinking there was something I had to come up with, when the key here was sincerely being interested."

It's so easy to engage that way. I don't care if you're in person, I don't care if you're on the Internet, I don't care if you're doing network marketing, I don't care if you're doing direct sales. The key thing is to not be so interested in trying to tell them about what your opportunity or what your facts are.

In the first place, you don't say, "Where are you now? Where are you wanting to get? Would you like to have a discussion online or offline about how something that we're engaged in," your partners whoever they are, "how what we're doing may be able to benefit where you said you'd like to go?"

It's kind of the basic syntax. I don't care, online or offline.

JED: That's the whole point, having a meaningful relationship, a meaningful conversation with the person that you're communicating with. I think really, that's what you just addressed here. That really is the key to anyone's success, regardless of where they are.

ARTEMIS: Right.

JED: Whether it's cultural differences, yes, there might be some small differences between cultural boundaries, but the general premise is that there really isn't. It's all human behavior.

ARTEMIS: Can we go into the covers a little bit on that one?

JED: Sure.

Why Can't We Say What We Mean?

ARTEMIS: The key thing that gets taxed here, and you've been through it, I've been through it, and most of the people that you and I interact with. The key thing that gets touched here is self-image and self-esteem. That's really what gets taxed.

I almost quit on my free enterprise business at about eight, ten weeks in, somewhere in there. I was trying to fire myself before any of them found out that I couldn't do what I set out to do. I was frightened, because it was all new and I thought it was going to be easy.

All of these different feelings and all of these different fears started coming up. I was thinking in a job mentality, so I was kind of like, "I'm going to take myself off the hook before any of these guys find out I can't do what I thought I could do."

I remember sitting on the sofa, and a gentleman who had been in the industry for at least ten years, he was very wise, said to me, "Artemis, first of all, you can always go back and do what you've always done."

Okay, that's nice, an agreement frame. Instead of saying you've got to or whatever, he sort of just said, "Look, you know you didn't have a bad life. You made more than six figures in corporate, so you can always go back. But, you can also go forward and learn what you've never known, and then create the life that most people only dream about."

That's when he had my full attention, because everything in me, as might be happening for you right now, everything in me jumped out, and I didn't say it verbally, but everything inside me was saying, "That's what I want."

Then he went on. I'm going to be honest; tears started streaming down my face. He said, "Look, this business faces everybody with what they're not good at."

The reason why people come to enter free enterprise, whether it's network marketing, whether it's Internet marketing, whether it's direct sales, whether it's online marketing, the reason people do that is they want to take their life to another level.

The whole point about when you want to take your life to another

Why Can't We Say What We Mean?

level is it's going to require learning all new things, especially in the beginning. It can be very disorienting, because you may not apply your previous strengths appropriately in these new industries right away.

It's almost like in the beginning, what you did know doesn't work, and you don't know what you don't know. It looks like, "Whoa!"

He said, "Look, this business faces everybody with what they're not good at, because everybody's trying to take their life from where it was to where they'd like it to be, which means that something they don't know is the key. Otherwise, they would already be there."

A very inner part of me was saying, "Yeah, okay. That makes really good sense."

The parts of me that were frightened, that I don't want to disappoint, and in any business or corporate environment, not knowing what you're doing is completely unacceptable. And you're absolutely going to get fired and you certainly don't ask questions. You certainly don't say you don't know it, whereas, in free enterprise there's a vulnerability that is required.

This is part of what you're allowing your audience to do, is to say, "Listen, engaging in coaching with people who have been where you want to go, being willing to show your under belly, and not being afraid to ask questions that in corporate wouldn't be appropriate."

To be honest, most of the time you're never going to show your vulnerabilities there.

JED: Oh, definitely not!

ARTEMIS: But here, that's important.

JED: Right, right.

ARTEMIS: If you don't show your vulnerabilities, if you're not willing to admit what you don't know, you're not likely to reach out to the people who can most help you.

The most beautiful thing about free enterprise that Jed and I both found is that, like we are to others, people are extremely generous with saying, "Come here."

Why Can't We Say What We Mean?

It's kind of a "Matrix" idea. If you took the red pill, then come over here and ask questions. In fact, it's required. Or, is it the blue pill in the "Matrix"? I forgot, now, which one it is.

JED: Yeah, I think it's the little blue pill.

ARTEMIS: It's the blue pill, right.

What I mean is, basically, if you're now in that place where you're saying, "I'd like to go out of bounds and I want to take my life to another level, yet there's part of me that is terrified, because there is a part of me that's aware that I don't know how to get from where I am to where I want to go," that's a beautiful thing.

JED: Let me ask you a couple more questions. If you were to look back, is there anything that you would do differently?

Perfect World!

ARTEMIS: If I had known then what I know now, I would have given myself more permission to relax in the learning.

I wouldn't have changed anything I didn't know, because you can't. I wouldn't have changed the learning curve. Of course, everybody would love to know everything instantly.

But, you know, the biggest thing is I was very answer oriented. I just needed to know what to do. I found that the first couple of years of free enterprise was where I got very proficient at the skills, and yet relaxing into who I was wasn't something that came as a result of logical answers and information.

I find that many of us are very hungry for the logical.

JED: Right, right

ARTEMIS: "Just give me the information, give me the facts, give me the o1 through 10, and you and I can both smile again."

JED: Gee, I'm very left-brained. What can I say?

ARTEMIS: To say that I got very proficient that first couple of years, and still the fear to relax into learning and being genuine, when I finally caught on to this idea:

Why Can't We Say What We Mean?

Hey, listen. The very people that I'm wanting to attract are going to go through exactly what I'm going through. My job is number one. Be my first experiment. I'm the first rep. I'm the first online customer. I'm the first direct sale customer.

What's my experience and am I willing to have fun in the process? Is this something that would capture my attention? Is this a fun interaction? If it didn't go well this time, what would I want to tell clients that I'm also going to attract to be business partners? They're going to go through it as well. What would I want to tell them?

I started to give myself room to say, "Ah. My job is to have a lot more fun in this, because who's going to want to come in any of these businesses as business partners, if it's as miserable as I've created it to be in my own mind?"

I think it was Mark Twain who said, "I've been through some terrible things in my life, some of which actually happened."

If I could go back and take one thing with me, it wouldn't be changing the things that I wasn't good at. It wouldn't be changing the number of transactions that I had to have to become good.

It would have been giving myself room to go through those transactions with a lot more ease and fun, and my attraction levels that happened after a couple of years would have been right then. I wasn't perfect later, but I was having fun and that was the key.

One of the things I have found that people are most hungry to learn from us is not what we are great at, but how did we get good at it.

"When you weren't good, what did you do?" That is the big question, not, "Oh, you're so good now."

It's like they want to know how you got from there to here. They are wanting to know that. Again, that really goes back to being willing to educate your expectations.

Why Can't We Say What We Mean?

Free enterprise requires different thinking. It requires different room, in terms of how you look at failure. It requires a completely different understanding of a learning curve, because there are many things that you're going to go back to learn that will strengthen what you've already known.

I'm thinking of Sampras, the tennis player. At a certain point, he became number one and he wanted to do something new with his ranking. He wanted to actually still become stronger. He hired a new coach. It's probably what many of us would do. It's not our parents, not necessarily our bosses, not necessarily our current friends, but new coaches who have experience.

This new coach said, "I don't know if you're going to want to do what I'm going to tell you, because I'm going to completely change everything and the way you do it. You will fall back in your ranking, and then you'll come back stronger than you've ever been. You can stay with what you know right now," very similar advice to what that gentleman said to me, "or you can be willing to change everything. I'm going to change the way you hold a tennis racket. I'm going to change the way you serve, the way you play the game, and while you're learning this new way, you're going to fall back in the rankings. You're not going to be as good at that stuff, but you'll come back stronger and you will hold number one."

Sampras had the courage to do it.

The question that Jed is opening up to you, and I would open up to you, is do you have the courage to give yourself that kind of room? You can come back stronger, financially is really the key, and then also personally to know things that very few people give themselves the chance to learn, because doubling their failure rate is unacceptable to many, although their desire is to get to places that only doubling your failure rate can get you.

JED: That brings me to this final question, and that's where I was so mechanical. I knew what I had to do. I would pick up the phone. I would take care of business. The one thing that was missing was my heart, was my gut, my soul, my heart, my spirit, the whole notion of really understanding what it was that I was

Why Can't We Say What We Mean?

trying to accomplish for the people I was involved with, and also for myself. I will bring this to the last question.

As you spend so much time with us, with coaching and training and guiding and helping people develop the skills, the knowledge, the basis, the foundation, all that becomes very taxing. What do you do to keep yourself healthy and fit, both physically and mentally, to maintain that relationship that is required for you to be an effective teacher and trainer and mentor?

ARTEMIS: That's a very powerful question that you're asking, Jed. One of the biggest changes in moving into free enterprise is that your mental fitness and your emotional mastery are very key to your financial mastery.

I would definitely say that mastery of the internal communications that you have with yourself, the external communication that you're developing with others to lead to that financial mastery. I didn't have that coming in, even with a sales background.

I'm going to be honest with you. The level to which I brought myself is completely different to the level to which corporate had developed me.

To give many of you just an understanding, probably in most jobs you use just about 25% to 35% of you. Most people bring 10% to 15%.

Those that bring 30% to 35% of who they are to their job, and I'm not talking time here, I'm not talking if you work an 18-hour day, I'm talking about truly what's inside you to bring, most people, 35%, would be people who are at the higher levels.

In free enterprise, you have got to be functioning at the 85% to 95% level to make money here. It's a completely different part of yourself that you've got to start making accessible.

There are some very specific things that I've learned to do, in terms of bringing myself in touch with the inspirations that drive me to want to offer the things that I offer.

There's a very different level of energy that goes out of you because, in fact, in really powerful

Why Can't We Say What We Mean?

        communications, what you and I are really doing is exchanging energy with others, which goes way beyond the words or the facts.

        In most business communications, people are taught to speak with the facts. In this arena, you and I are really going to be learning to exchange energy. Nothing I have ever done before has ever required that energy exchange. The key thing is that I do have to do things to have energy coming into me in order for it to come out of me, as in the past couple of days. We've had a very intensive three days together.

JED: Very much so.

ARTEMIS: I know now there are things that I will do today for refreshment, specifically not just resting, but specific things that you do.

        There are many things on the Internet that are very inspirational. YouTube has been a very amazing vehicle for bringing many things that can waken, and I think many of us assume that we should wake up and just be able to go to work.

Copyright © 2008. Jed A. Reay. All rights reserved.

What I want to say to you is visualization, learning how to go into the workshop of your imagination, and Jed and I can assist you with some things with this in the future. These things are very key.

The way that you deal with yourself physically, and even though I have dealt in health for the last eight years, right now I'm in the midst of doing that to a whole other level.

In order to make yourself available in those ways, you do have an energy exchange. Many people come into this business and they'll come for coaching, and the first thing that is easy for any seasoned person, and I can easily see, is it's as if you got in your car with a quarter tank of gas.

We're in Dallas right now, and you said, "I'm going to California." And you call me from a few hours away and say, "I don't know what happened. I'm exhausted."

"Let's look at your gas tank."

You're like, "I don't know why it's empty. I don't know why there's not enough."

I say, "Okay, go to the gas station."

Why Can't We Say What We Mean?

You go. You fill it up and then you call me from the other side of Arizona and you go, "Oh, my god! It happened again, Artemis."

You know now that makes immediate sense to us. But when it comes to energy and when it comes to fueling your passion and your vision, most of us are not used to doing that on a daily or an hourly basis, depending on what you are really working with. That's a whole skill level in and of itself.

There are a couple of resources that Jed and I will recommend to you.

I would love to talk a little bit about it with you. Even though you were going to make this the final question, can we explore one other area?

JED: Sure, you bet. Thank you.

ARTEMIS: Jed has shared with me that many of you are in network marketing and direct sales. When it comes to communicating over the phone or in person, one of the key things is that energy that you actually bring to the phone. It can be years that people can be so disappointed, because they get on the phone and they basically just talk normally.

Let's say that I was a performer and I'm talking now like this with Jed. But if I was in a theatre, there would be no way that this would be enough to project out to the back of the row in the theatre. There would be no way.

If I was an opera singer, then singing in the shower is one thing, but an opera singer, in order to do it, has to sing from a completely different place. They're not singing from the same place that I would sing if I'm humming along with the radio or a CD.

You and I, as communicators, need to understand that there's a whole different level. I have to bring all of me. I have to bring all of me, not just my logic, whether I'm on the phone or I'm on the Internet, even in the words I might choose, if I'm doing online marketing.

There are things that draw people towards you. Many times we don't realize that when you go to use your whole body, when you go to express yourself more fully, when you go to actually speak from your passion, it

Why Can't We Say What We Mean?

feels funny if you've never done it before. It feels over the top. It feels like that's not appropriate. And yet, you will continue to get mediocre, if not downright poor results when you don't do that.

JED: I can attest to that.

ARTEMIS: I think probably everybody who's listening, and I can certainly confirm that as well. In the first couple of years that I was doing network marketing, the gentleman that was one of the people at the top would say to me, "You sound good, Artemis, but you still sound kind of salesy." I didn't know what he meant until I finally started speaking from passion.

Why are you and I here? Why have you been drawn to your particular business or profession that you're pursuing? What is it that you are truly hungry to understand from Jed and Artemis? What is that?

As you learn some things and you take it in intellectually and it still doesn't really work, I'll be honest with you. You'll take it in, you'll try it and it still won't work. You might get frustrated, you might get mad. You might get downright furious.

Those things will drive you to get a little deeper. Anything that doesn't make you quit will make you drive a little deeper and bring a little more of you out here.

"Maybe now when I come to Jed and Artemis, I might ask the same exact question, but I'm a little more open to listening. Maybe the rules of my life still make me engage only intellectually. I go back and I say, 'Okay, now I understand what they said a little better.'"

But you still have those rules that make you play it safe.

I used to joke with my husband and say, "You wanted to make $20 million, but it took a wild and crazy Greek girl to get you out of your physics, engineering mind, or you would have played it too safe."

Much of what we bring to each other, what he has taught me is a steadiness of confidence that was natural to him, that was completely not natural to me. Self-esteem was key. Really engaging and realizing that my internal dialogue, I never had to address at corporate, Jed, I never had to address it.

Why Can't We Say What We Mean?

JED: I didn't either.

ARTEMIS: Some really bad stuff was going on in here and I made six figures. Nobody cared to ask me to straighten it out. I couldn't get anything going on in free enterprise, in network marketing or direct sales. I couldn't get anything going on until I straightened that out.

Somehow that incongruence, that conflictedness, somehow that communicated something that I didn't realize that was more powerful than words that I was saying.

If some of these areas are touching home with you, then I would really encourage you to take Jed and me up on coming and spending a little bit more time. Whether it's a teleseminar with us, whether it's a webinar that we end up doing, or whether you end up doing some one-on-one coaching. I would encourage you to come closer.

JED: I would agree.

ARTEMIS: Realize that this journey that you're on is intellectually only going to be the first place. Learning happens in two stages. One is where you and I go out and acquire information. That's what you're doing now.

Stage two is going to be where you go to apply it in the game, and that's where powerful coaches can compress a lot of time for you.

Initially, people want to spend a lot of time to make money, but you guys are at the stage now where you want to know that we all invest money in order to buy back our time.

Be open, double your failure rate. Be hungry to engage with coaching at deeper levels.

Jed, it's been such a privilege being with you.

JED: I can't tell you how much I appreciate you, Artemis. As I've said, the last three days have been a very, very, very special time for me. We talked about that just briefly, that things were mechanical. You have a system of the way you train us. That process that first time was very mechanical, and I didn't get it.

ARTEMIS: Yeah.

JED: But I did this week. I did, and I have to say that I love you for it. And,

Why Can't We Say What We Mean?

Blair, you're a lucky man; I've got to tell you. She's a very special person, and I want to thank you very much for the time you've given me and my audience. It's great advice.

ARTEMIS: You're welcome.

You guys will smile because my website is www.paidmydues.net. If you're wanting to pay your dues, then let's connect together with Jed. It's great being with you.

JED: Thank you.

Copyright © 2008. Jed A. Reay. All rights reserved.

CHAPTER 9:
INTERVIEW WITH
TIM MCKEE

Mr. Tim McKee

Tim McKee is a successful Internet entrepreneur and award-winning producer, director, and editor for NBC, CNN and TBS with 25 years of national advertising experience. He has earned a variety of accolades for his work, including two Emmys and two Telly Awards.

Tim is the creator of the EDM process, **Emotion Directed Marketing**. Through his company EasyVideoTools.com he teaches online marketers how to create and distribute strategically designed video content with Web 2.0 distribution, and is building a reputation among online marketers for his ability to move a start-up brand and its entrepreneur from relative obscurity to social marketing prominence through simple, step-by-step video marketing.

Why Can't We Say What We Mean?

Prior to that, Tim was VP and managing partner for NewsProNet, one of the largest national syndicators of enterprise, investigative, and topical news content for ABC, NBC, and CBS and its online properties. His stellar list of clients reads like a "Who's Who" of broadcast and business industries.

Contact Tim at tim.mckee@easyvideotools.com for information on how **EDM** can move your business forward.

INTERVIEW

JED: Well, hello. This is Jed Reay coming from the beautiful Northwest with another segment, another chapter in the book, *Why Can't We Say What We Mean? Developing Meaningful Business Relationships Through Effective Communication.*

I have the great privilege to introduce to you an individual that comes from a personal background of mine, someone that I know personally and that I have great esteem for. I asked him to come on and give his insights into this topic, Mr. Tim McKee.

Tim comes with a plethora of pedigree: two Emmys, two Tellys, and a retiring producer from CNN out of the Atlanta office. Can we give a warm welcome for Mr. Tim McKee?

TIM: Hey, Jed. Good to be with you today.

JED: Thank you very, very much. You have a very unique background in communication, in that you've spent in excess of 25 years in the media industry communicating to millions and millions and millions of people. So, it's very appropriate that you are a part of this project.

Let me just start off by asking you, if you were to give us your impression of communication in developing a meaningful relationship in a business arena, what would you say? What does that mean to you?

TIM: That's a great question. Actually, it's a very appropriate question to ask. What I see, and certainly what I've seen over my career, I think the key word here is trust. In all relationships, in order to have meaningful relationships, what needs to exist is a mutual trust between people.

In order to have trust, you have to get to know the other person, whether that is a business partner, a

Why Can't We Say What We Mean?

	prospect, or whether they're standing next to you or across the planet. All successful business relationships are based on trust. We don't get to a win/win, everybody wins situation unless there is this trust between us.
JED:	It's interesting that you say that, because there's a common theme that's running through all of these interviews that I've done. Isn't it interesting that's the common theme, that in order to have an effective, healthy communication and relationship there has to be mutual trust?
	Some of the others have said we're always looking to what the other person wants to achieve out of this interaction. In order for you to make a connection, you have to be willing to listen.
	That being said, it brings me to my second question.
	During a conversation that you'll have with, say, one person or multiple people, it's rather difficult over the phone, but it still can be done. What cues do you have that you're connected, that someone is connecting with you and that you're

connecting with them? What kind of cues do you pay attention to, do you key in on?

TIM: That's a great question. If you're an observer of human behavior, you can see these cues and you can hear them. You don't actually have to see somebody. So much of our work happens on the Internet. We work with video. We're able to give our prospects or potential business partners cues into what we're thinking, into what our core values, our integrity, our honesty is because they can see us. But we can't see them.

There are a number of cues that I look for. When we talk to a person, maybe 40% of the communication really comes through with the words. The rest of that communication comes through in body language.

I know that when I'm talking to somebody and they're looking me in the eye and they engage with me by looking at me, I know that they are interested, that they are relating to what I am saying.

The way that I approach business communications and business relationships, in general, is really

Why Can't We Say What We Mean?

similar to a dating situation. Think back when you were a teenager, in your early twenties when you were courting your wife. She had to learn to trust you, and you had to learn to trust her.

The way we do that is we share more and more about ourselves, we share more and more about our history. And in the telling of that history, we learn what core values each of us has.

When I'm developing a relationship with new partners or new prospects, I have to share a lot about myself. Because what I want from them is honesty and integrity, I'm obligated and committed to giving that relationship my honesty and my integrity. That's what I'm looking to attract into my relationships and my business, and into all my relationships, for that matter.

The cues that I receive when I'm giving parts of my story and learning about them is when I see them listening intently, when I see them adding parts of their own story when I tell my story. I see the nods. When I see them sitting up in the chair and the eyes wide open and the subtle nod, I know that we're communicating.

There are plenty of times when I'm sharing my story and asking questions to them that I get lots of those signals, just in the fact that they share honestly and openly. I don't hear a lot of nos.

I know that on that subconscious level where we really make decisions, where we really communicate and we've made a connection.

JED: Isn't that interesting? What you've just said is keying in on several of the other components that, even without asking them ahead of time, other questions that I have for you. We may change the direction that we're going.

Give me a little bit of an idea of what you think the characteristics and the abilities are to be an effective communicator, assuming that they're not innate. We didn't pop out and the doctor slapped you on the fanny and you're a born communicator, right? There are certain abilities, certain characteristics, just a certain way about the way someone carries themselves to be an effective

Why Can't We Say What We Mean?

communicator. Can you talk about those?

TIM: Sure. I believe that we are all born as perfect communicators. What happens to a lot of us is we forget it, and we need to rediscover it. But at our very core we all have really the same set of needs. We have the same desires to connect, to belong, to be valued in relationships, and to make a contribution in this world. That's a universal set of values that we all have.

When we communicate on that level, the words come naturally. Ninety percent of it is to share with honesty and integrity, to share your truth. Don't judge the words or your story, because it's your story, it's your words. The watchwords here are really integrity and honesty. I believe when you share on that level, you really can't share the wrong thing.

JED: Isn't that interesting? It's fascinating that you say that, because I really, truly do believe that we did have that. You can see it when you look into a baby's face, into their eyes, into their spirit. Look at a very, very young child that knows only to accept everything that they see in the world.

They don't know that they shouldn't do this or shouldn't do that, or shouldn't say this or shouldn't say that. The old adage that I remember as a young person was from the mouth of babes. Isn't that ironic that you share that with us?

TIM: Absolutely. What happens, Jed, is I believe that unless we have developed skills, and here's the skill set that one has to develop, and that is the ability to forgive oneself, the ability to move on. We all make mistakes.

We all have history and we all have some baggage. It's that baggage that gets in the way of effectively communicating with honesty and integrity. The first step, if we're going to put a step system to this in the process, is let go of the baggage.

Let it go. Let go of the past and engage in present day. Be present with your prospects, or your partner or your wife or your kids. It really goes for any situation. Be present and let go. Let go of that baggage. It has no relevance. It just drags the

Why Can't We Say What We Mean?

possibility for successful business communication down.

We're in a culture that you would agree supports a level of dishonesty, because we place money at the top of our value system. We tend to do anything and say anything in order to get that. Rather than value honesty as the prime, we'll value money. We've all done this. I've done it as well. It never leads to a good relationship.

When I can be here and be totally present with you without the baggage of my past, without shame, guilt and hidden motives, and come with a true, serving heart, how can I solve the issue that you're currently having without wanting something in return?

Then trust starts. Trust is absolutely the base component in successful relationships and in sales, in general. If we don't have that trust, we don't have sales.

JED: It's so true. It's almost like the good news newspaper. I'm thrilled. This is the most exhilarating thing that I have ever done in my life. This project, this whole idea of interacting with some very, very competent, influential people from around the country, it's just truly, truly fascinating when you look to others first for their advice and guidance and for their direction, and lo and behold look at what's transpired.

There is this blossoming project, this blossoming flower that has just grown, all because of other people stepping out and offering their assistance.

You addressed the fourth and fifth question. Can you give our audience some simple steps to help them improve their communication?

You've really addressed a lot of those. I think what I'd like to do is have you elaborate a little bit on the current business model that you're working in. You've kind of gone out and done some freelance video, some audio, and you're starting a new company and just gone live. You're in your second month now of a new project, and it would be nice if you would share a little bit about it.

TIM: Sure, I'd love to. Thanks for asking. I've been in broadcast television for 25 years, and during the course of that time, I've had an opportunity to

Why Can't We Say What We Mean?

identify why people make buying decisions, essentially.

I did quite a bit of study on how the brain processes information, in terms of making a decision to buy, and came up with a process called EDM, Emotional Directed Marketing.

What that's about is talking to that part of the brain that makes the decisions to buy. It's the primitive part of our brain. It's the reptilian part of our brain, and this is the one that has fight or flight and makes decisions based on what's good and bad. It works in very black and white terms.

We've known for years in advertising and television how this works. What I've done is develop a simple set of tools to teach people how to use this process to create effective video to market their service and products online. Essentially, the idea is to pull people out of the noise level and have them get massive attention with just a whisper.

We take people through our workshop, which is a six-session workshop that we do once a month, to teach them how to build effective, strategically built video, and then how to use some simple Web 2.0 social marketing strategies to get massive exposure; it's Google organic page one ranking, get it quickly to build their brand and get exposure for their message. That's essentially what we do.

There's no question that video has come of age on the Internet. Everywhere you look you see video attached with whatever message, whatever content is out there, and now is the time. Now is the time to build your brand with video on the Internet.

In fact, I would go as far as to say if you're not doing that, you're going to have a very tough go of it as an online marketer on the Internet.

JED: I can personally attest to being a part of the first class. I am just enthralled with the information that I learned. I've been putting up videos on the Internet for some time prior to taking your class, and I was just thrilled with the whole process. I know that as you grow and develop this, it's truly going to grow into something very, very wonderful. That's pretty amazing. Thank you.

Why Can't We Say What We Mean?

TIM: It's a lot of fun. It's very cool to be out there doing something I love and seeing people take information and get results, and get good results. That's very exciting.

JED: Talk a moment about what you think of your personal strengths, your characteristics, your ability, your personality. What is it that drives you?

TIM: I learned a long time ago that I'm a good listener. I learn a lot both by what people say and what they don't say. So I've learned to be a good student of human nature. I love to observe people and I love to observe human behavior.

One of my core strengths is I listen well. I listen to what people are saying and what they're not saying to get the true message. I know that all of us walk around with two identities. We have an outer identity and an inner identity.

We have that outer identity, which is what we see every day, what we present to each other every day. And we have that inner identity, which is our real core desires, our real core beliefs, like, "I'd rather be living on the beach than sitting here in a small cubicle." We all have those desires.

I know that most people are subconsciously motivated by that true desire, and that's the person that I want to speak to. I know how to listen for that. I believe I've developed a pretty well-honed sense of content creation for video, and I think I'm pretty good at making effective video.

I think the third component is I'm a good teacher. I enjoy teaching people. I have a tremendous love for teaching people.

Those three things have come together. It's taken me 50 years to kind of figure out those three things, but they've come together and I'm happy and I'm having a good time. I'm having a really good time in life.

JED: That's what's so fascinating about this discussion. I've come in contact with some very, very good, special people through this whole process. Honestly, I have to give you, personally, some credit.

You have guided me and helped me along in this process and given some direction as to how to make this

Why Can't We Say What We Mean?

happen. It's just fascinating to me as to how all this process just all of a sudden became real, all because of a few very effective conversations, very open and very straightforward, honest, and direct communications about what it is that I wanted to try and accomplish.

That provided other people a stage on which to share their personal experiences in communication and having this conversation.

As a final question, having effective conversations and being involved with other human beings on a personal level can be a little taxing. It definitely can.

As a teacher, trainer, mentor, and human change agent, you have a powerful influence on those of us that you come in contact with. What do you do to maintain your vision, your direction, your thirst, your hunger? What is it that you do to keep yourself going?

TIM: There is the golden question there, Jed. I think that life is a tapestry made up of a lot of elements. The key is to do the best of one's ability to stay in balance.

	If I feel I'm getting pulled too much in one direction, I need to back off, I need to relax. The way that I recharge my batteries is I love to run, I play music, and I play piano and guitar. Those are some creative releases for me.
	The key here is balance. I can sit and edit for hours and hours and hours, and the next thing I know, it's 3:00 a.m.
JED:	You get carried away, huh?
TIM:	Yeah. Balance is very, very important to me, to stay balanced with what I put into my body, both food and thought that I put into my body.
	Keep the first things first. I like to get up in the morning, and the first thing I do, generally, is take a run, maybe have a little breakfast, a little prayer and meditation, and then immediately dive into my most productive time of the day.
	I have about two hours late morning that I get 80% of my income-producing activities done. Then I take a break. I may take a nap, I may go for a walk, do something, read, do some writing.

Why Can't We Say What We Mean?

I have to hit at the peak of my energy, the number one thing. I have to keep those going. That's how I stay charged.

JED: Isn't that fascinating? All of these interviews in this book speak to exactly that same tone. There's prayer and meditation. There's self-reflection. Everything I'm gathering from all of these people so far that are a part of this project, have all said the same thing. Fascinating, amazing.

TIM: True. They all teach each other.

JED: Tim McKee, I can only say that I have been blessed greatly by knowing you. I can say publicly that I love you and I am very, very grateful for your involvement in my life. You have helped me and I can't begin to thank you enough.

Are there any parting words that you may have that you'd like to send to our audience?

TIM: I want to throw some big congratulations your way too, Jed. You've stepped up into some large areas in your life, and I'm very, very proud of you for what you're doing and the service that you're bringing to others with this project.

Buddy, you've been a huge part of my life. You've given me guidance and helped me out on a regular basis. You're a huge part of my life too, so it goes both ways. That is a successful relationship.

JED: Amen.

TIM: I think with those words, that's it.

JED: That's a wrap!

Why Can't We Say What We Mean?

CHAPTER 10: INTERVIEW WITH LYNN PIERCE

Ms. Lynn Pierce

Lynn Pierce is known as **The Success Architect** who, for more than 25 years, has taught people how to combine business and personal development to reach the pinnacle of success and live the life of their dreams.

Lynn is the author of *Breakthrough To Success: 19 Keys to Mastering Every Area of Your Life* and a #1 bestselling co-author of *Wake-up... Live the Life You Love.* Lynn is the founder of one of the most exciting and informative annual events for women entrepreneurs, Women's Business Empowerment Summit.

www.jedthecommunicator.com

Her personal and professional development systems help business owners get three times the results in half the time at one-tenth of the effort. Lynn personally mentors people who have achieved success in their career and now want to do something more personally fulfilling to them – living their passion and life purpose.

Visit www.lynnpierce.com for Lynn's "Breakthrough To Success" step-by-step roadmap that takes you from wishing and trying to achieving in no time.

INTERVIEW

JED: Good morning, everyone. This is Jed Reay coming to you live with another wonderful, wonderful interview. I want to introduce a very special guest, Lynn Pierce.

Lynn is known as the "Success Architect" and for the past 30 years has taught thousands of speakers, authors, coaches, consultants, sales teams, and independent entrepreneurs how to tremendously increase their income.

I've asked Lynn to come on and help us out with this project. *Why Can't We Say What We Mean?* is the title of the book and it's about developing

Why Can't We Say What We Mean?

meaningful relationships in business through effective communication.

Lynn has been gracious enough to join us and tell us a little bit about her philosophies. Lynn, welcome.

LYNN: Thank you, Jed. I'm happy to be here.

JED: This whole phenomenon of the human communication, human connection, from my perspective, is something that is not an innate behavior. When we pop out and the doctor slaps our fanny, we're not born communicators.

From your perspective, what does it mean to communicate and develop a meaningful relationship in a business arena?

LYNN: I think the key word there, at least from my perspective, is meaningful. Most of our conversations that we have are superficial, and at best, they're on a conscious but surface level. You never really get into a deep, meaningful conversation with someone, unless there's a trigger that shows up, or unless it's someone that you already feel safe with.

You have those kinds of conversations with your close friends or your family, but typically not in business, because for some reason we've created this distance between ourselves and the people we communicate with in business.

To really have meaningful relationships and meaningful conversations, you have to get beyond that surface level of questions that you're asking.

JED: Isn't that fascinating? It just brought up a situation that happened to me yesterday, and that leads me kind of back into the second question. I sent out an email to my entire personal list asking for them to update some personal data in case they've moved. I haven't done it for many, many years.

I got a kickback from somebody saying, "Hey, take me off of your daily motivational."

I thought, "Did I understand what he said? Remove me."

I had to actually make a phone call in order to really understand what it was. It says, "Please remove me," but my question didn't have anything

Why Can't We Say What We Mean?

to do with my daily motivational, so I had to actually call him to figure that out. Isn't that interesting?

This next question kind of helps people like you and me make a connection. For example, if you were to have a conversation with one person or more at the same time, what are the dynamics of that conversation that tell you that you're connecting, that you know what they want and they know what you want?

Obviously, the telephone is difficult for you and me to make real connection, but it's better than a voicemail or an email. In life, when you're doing these interactions or having these conversations in a live situation, how do you know that you're making a connection?

LYNN: First of all, it isn't as different as you may think it is to do it by phone or by email, because in the last few years, I would say that the majority of the interaction that I do is through teleseminars, where there may be some degree of interaction, but for the most part it's just me talking.

I have no idea what's going on, on the other end. I'm not sure if anybody's even there when I mute that line and I'm teaching. It's different to communicate that way. And then through email, you only have their responses to rely on. But with blogging, that's a little more interactive.

Whether it's in person or through your blog or through maybe Q&A on a teleseminar, the things are very similar, where they're agreeing with you. Somehow you're getting that impression, either over the phone or through comments that are posted to your blog, that they're agreeing with you. They're letting you know that they feel heard. They feel understood.

In what you would call a "sales presentation" where there's a product or service that you're having a conversation about, somewhere towards the end of that conversation the potential client is actually parroting back to you your own words that you've used earlier in the conversation, and they don't even realize it.

You've connected on a deep level and they have that trust and that rapport with you. They're using your words to relay back to you how your

Why Can't We Say What We Mean?

product or service can help them. You know that you've reached them and you have that connection at that point.

It also comes from learning how to ask those deeper levels of questions below that surface level, the second and third level questions. A lot of times if you're having a conversation with someone to get to what their real needs and desires are, to have that real conversation, you're taking them someplace that they may not have gone before, themselves.

You're asking them for answers that you're going to have to help them to access, because they're their subconscious desires. But really, you make the buying decision.

You don't know that and they don't know that unless you can help them access that and bring it to the surface. So in some way, they're telling you the truth, the truth that they may not have even been aware of, because no one's ever asked them those questions before. That's where you have that real connection.

JED: Isn't that amazing? It really, truly is that simple. It's oftentimes that when

I speak personally with either a new business client or a potential customer that there are some concerns, because the type of business that I do requires you to have the ability to communicate.

A lot of people use that same scenario as the word sales. "I'm not a salesman. I can't sell."

It's interesting, because it's just about having a conversation and making a connection. That kind of leads me to this next question.

I alluded to it earlier in the conversation about innate, whether or not being a communicator or being able to carry on a conversation is an innate behavior or ability. Let's get your opinion.

LYNN: First of all, I think that I spent 25 years of my career in sales and doing sales training mostly of actual sales people. Even they, to a large extent, didn't consider themselves to be salespeople. It was just a job that they happen to have that involved sales.

They felt just as uncomfortable with that whole connotation, because in the back of their mind they're

Why Can't We Say What We Mean?

thinking of a bad movie, like used cars, or one of those things where it's more like a con man.

My entire career has been, "That's not what we're talking about. That's the negative side, but that's not the real side."

I think it was Michael Gerber who said, "You may think you're in this business or that business, but the only business anybody is in, is sales. If you don't sell whatever it is, you don't have a business."

One of the things that people really have to get, besides getting past that whole connotation of not being a salesperson and just look at it as if nobody is a salesperson, is most people will either talk to a potential client as a stranger and have them at what they call "arms length" transactions. What would make you think that's a good thing?

Or they talk to them on too close of a level that makes the other person uncomfortable, like if you're treating them as family, they're going, "Oh, I don't know you that well. You're getting a little too close for my comfort."

Somewhere in between is that friend level. You're being friendly without crossing the line of being their friend. When you cross the line from being friendly to friend, they can say no to a friend, and the friend will understand any excuse they feel like coming up with.

If you're friendly, you've closed that gap from talking to a stranger, and yet not gone too far on the other side. That would be one thing.

The other thing is learning how to effectively communicate with all four personality styles, and taking into account the fact that they not only take in information differently, they interact differently, and they absolutely use different criteria for making decisions.

When you're thinking that you're disconnecting with someone and that they don't like you, that you said something wrong or they are saying no to your product or your service, chances are it's just the way that the presentation took place. The communication between the two of you was not a good fit for their personality.

Why Can't We Say What We Mean?

If you came back to them with that same conversation tailored in a way that they could really take in the information and connect in a way that they needed to be talked to, and showed them the benefits that really appeal to their personality style, and then help them to arrive at the decision in the way they need to get there, you have a completely different conclusion.

People go around basically chasing their tales, changing this or changing that, when that's probably not it at all. It has nothing to do with you or your product. It's just the style of communication you're using isn't a fit for that particular person.

JED: That's a perfect segue into the next two questions, and we'll just ask them as one big question.

Are there some resources or simple steps that you can give our audience to develop some communication skills? Can you give us some advice on some simple steps, places to go? And then also, obviously, your website provides a service and you provide a service. I'd like you to elaborate a little bit on that, maybe some simple steps that our audience can grasp, so that they can help them communicate better.

LYNN: The first thing I would say is listen from your heart with the intent of being of service to that person, really be listening from that place, listening for what they're not saying, for the underlying needs and desires that they have. That will help you learn how to ask those deeper level questions.

For the majority of people, that's something that has to be learned, and it takes some active practice. There are a few people that are just naturally inquisitive and they just go deeper and deeper and deeper. That's just who they are. But for the majority of people, it's an acquired skill.

The other thing is create a powerful presentation for your product or service, and then work on converting it into what works best for each of those four personality styles. That's what I've created, a system that does all of these things that we're talking about, that puts it into a very simple step-by-step process of creating that presentation in a way that flows in a productive order that will take people to the nature conclusion of

Why Can't We Say What We Mean?

"Yes" at the end of the conversation, and then also helps you to convert it to all four personality styles, so that you're asking the right questions in the right way that will really connect with those people.

That program is called "Getting To YES Without Selling," and it's available in two different levels, a quick start version and a full version on my website. It's whatever level of knowledge, however deep you choose to go.

I would say don't just focus on business and marketing books, courses, seminars. Personal development and a person's psychology is the key to, I think, everything in life. It's the key to your personal success, because you've got to understand yourself on a deeper and deeper level all the time.

Introspection is hugely important, because you can't communicate clearly if you don't know where you're communicating from. And then also, the more you understand yourself, the more you understand and empathize with other people, and that deepens that connection.

Copyright © 2008. Jed A. Reay. All rights reserved.

I think the business tools are secondary to that personal connection that you develop.

JED: I have to comment. It's interesting, in this process that I've gone through in doing these interviews with a cross-section of very successful entrepreneurs about this particular topic, that is probably the most common links that link us all together is what you just said.

Introspection, number one, and number two is a genuine listening interest in what others are saying and not saying in the conversation.

It's just amazing to me that here's a group of people that don't know each other, for the most part, some of them do, some of them don't. But for them all to basically articulate the same message is quite fascinating to me.

It's just like that neuro-linguistic program, that if I say something four times within a very short period of time, that must mean that it's important. Obviously, if all 12 of these people have basically said the same thing, I think it's pretty important.

Why Can't We Say What We Mean?

That leads us onto the strengths, but I want to go back. Lynn's website is www.lynnpierce.com and you can get all of the mechanical information that Lynn was talking about from the website.

I would agree that introspection and having a centered heart and soul is extremely important in a conversation.

Looking back, if you had to do it all over again, would you change anything?

LYNN: I think I would give myself a break. When I think back to when I started and I was 22 years-old and my self-esteem at that point was still extremely low, I had so many inner struggles that I was dealing with. My passion since high school has been psychology books, and then progressing into self-help books, is what they called them back then.

I was working really hard to be a better person, and I really thought, at that point, that I was having that level of conversation with people. But looking back, I wasn't equipped as who I was at that point to really have that conversation. And yet, I was having a totally different conversation than anybody else I knew, and my sales reflected that.

It doesn't matter where you're starting from, just having the conscious focus of wanting to have that conversation. And then as you learn more, you can do more and you can go deeper. Just taking that on and saying, "That is my goal," will immediately transform the level of conversation that you're having.

That would probably be the biggest thing, to let it go. And as you learn more, you'll do better. Just have that in front of you.

JED: It's really interesting, because as I age, I'm becoming more aware of the impact that I personally have on the world, but more so, the impact that I have on myself. I've always been introspective, but never for any length of time, or never for any significant mind growth, is the way I look at it, until just recently.

For me, my introspection is more in the lines of devoted meditation on a daily basis, once or twice a day sitting and doing very specific meditations. It's quite amazing how I've been able to improve my ability

Why Can't We Say What We Mean?

to interact with the world around me and people like yourself, and some of the things that have happened.

That kind of brings us somewhat to a conclusion, but there are some other things that are just as important to what you said about what you believe are important components for our audience.

You're communicating at a very high level when you share or teach somebody or mentor somebody, and it has from years of experience that you bring forth information and guidance to help someone.

With that in mind, what would you suggest we do in the area of consciousness, with regard to what I just said about meditation? It's my belief, personally, that that heightens my ability to communicate with the world, with other people. I'm more focused on what it is they are trying to communicate to me and what I'm trying to communicate to them.

Does that play a part?

LYNN: Absolutely. Daily spiritual practice and mediation is, I believe, the foundation of everything in your life. It's impossible to sustain success long-term. You can always create success, you can create money, but then you get one of these "made-it, lost it, had to make it again" stories.

To sustain it long-term, that's the foundation. The first product that I ever created, *Change One Thing, Change Your Life*, is what I call a "personal transformation system." What it is, is 40 days of lessons and questions that you answer. Basically, they're meditations that I ciphered through every 40 days. And I created that back in 2001 and I still do it every single day.

I think that and other spiritual work that I do every single morning when I wake up not only sets the tone for my day, but it sets the foundation for my life and the place from which I communicate from my soul to someone else.

The other thing that keeps me going throughout the day is living in a place that I've created, an environment that feeds me, that energizes me, that once again speaks to my soul. So I go out into nature, into my yard, and I look at the view.

I'm moving to Maui next week and I'm going to be looking at a different

Why Can't We Say What We Mean?

>view than I'm looking at this week; but creating that space in your environment where you work.
>
>And then for me, also my dogs, my friends that I connect with, those are the things that fill me up, because when I communicate with people, I prepare myself to deliver from the highest place I can be and to deliver 100%. That does take a lot of energy, if you're coming from that place. You do have to take care of yourself and have that awareness around yourself.

JED: It's interesting, because you answered even the last question. The last and final question is what do you do to keep your tank full? And so, you are doing what it is that you teach. Every single day you, yourself, are a student of your own teachings.

LYNN: I think everybody teaches what they need to learn on an ongoing basis.

JED: That's an interesting way of looking at it.

LYNN: That whatever it is that turns out to be your passion is usually something that you've been excited about learning, and then you teach you. Sometimes you're continually teaching as you're continually learning.

The growth process never ends. As you learn more, you teach more. When I do those lessons, I don't even look at it as something I created. I look at it as that's what I'm supposed to get for that day. That's what I'm supposed to focus on for that day.

The fact that I originally wrote those words on that page has nothing to do with it, as far as I'm concerned.

JED: Lynn, you have been a tremendous part of this project, and I can't begin to thank you enough.

You can find Lynn at www.lynnpierce.com

Lynn, I look forward to a long and productive and healthy relationship between the two of us, and I thank you very, very much for the time that you've given.

LYNN: I've really enjoyed having this conversation with you. I'm just kind of buzzing sitting here, because I love talking about this stuff. I have to

Why Can't We Say What We Mean?

tell you, when you were talking about the things that we have in common, I have a vision of all of us that are involved with this with you getting together and having a conversation on a whole different level that might lead to something huge.

JED: I like that vision. That's cool!

LYNN: I see that, I really see that. Think about that.

JED: I'm very pleased to have met you, and again, I look forward to a long and healthy relationship between the two of us. Thank you very much.

LYNN: Thank you.

Copyright © 2008. Jed A. Reay. All rights reserved.

www.jedthecommunicator.com

CHAPTER 11: INTERVIEW WITH STEPHEN PIERCE

Mr. Stephen Pierce

Stephen Pierce is recognized as one of the **world's leading Internet Marketers and Business Optimization Strategists** whose name is synonymous with success. Stephen wears several hats when it comes to his businesses. Not only is he the **CEO of Stephen Pierce International, Inc.** and the mastermind behind **DTAlpha**, he is a coach, a facilitator, and a Certified Accelerated Innovation Trainer.

Stephen is considered one of today's top authorities on creating rapid wealth using the Internet and serves as keynote speaker at events across the globe, from the U.S. to the U.K., from Australia to Asia, and everywhere in between. His

Why Can't We Say What We Mean?

instruction is based on time-tested, proven, solid techniques coupled with his motivational, humorous, and down-to-earth method of delivery.

Having personally overcome obstacles of homelessness, bankruptcy and being shot, Stephen instinctively knows how to zero in on solutions to business and personal challenges with an instinctive ability to help others tap into the ideas, strategies, and knowledge they need to reach success in their business and personal lives.

Contact support@piercesupport.com or Google **Stephen Pierce** for information about his websites, programs, conference and speaking schedules, products and FREE items.

INTERVIEW

JED: Good morning, this is Jed Reay. I'm coming to you remotely, and we have a special guest on the line. As you're aware, I'm in the process of putting together a book, *Why Can't We Say What We Mean? Developing Meaningful Relationships Through Effective Communication*.

Today, I have the privilege of introducing to you Stephen Pierce. Stephen is an internationally known speaker and an Internet marketing superstar. Welcome, Stephen.

Stephen, you've done this by building relationships on the Internet. How do you overcome the impersonal effects with email and being able to reach your target market?

STEPHEN: Thank you, Jed. It's nice to be here, and that's a great question. I think one of the things to realize is that email isn't necessarily what I consider to be a sole channel for communication. But I think it's good at supplementing other communication channels that you want to use.

For example, if you and I already have a personal relationship and we already have personal dialogue, then the emails that we exchange are going to help support and supplement our communication in our relationship.

If I don't have a relationship with you, and this is from a marketing aspect, and I'm looking to building one, email may be the thing that initiates the relationship, makes us aware of each other, brings us into contact, at which point I'll open up and start doing other forms of communication with that particular person, be it on the telephone or

Why Can't We Say What We Mean?

webinars or teleseminars, live events, or whatever.

I think that email can be impersonal, but the character of email, I think, is influenced by understanding the level of relationship that it is we have with different people.

I think it's really important to understand that solely using email isn't necessarily a great thing. It's a supplement in existing relationships and adds to the communication, or it can help initiate new relationships, in which you then expand the channels of communication.

JED: Wonderful, okay. That makes a lot more sense. Can you give our audience some simple advice to improve their abilities to communicate and connect with someone via the Internet that they need to connect with, in order to move forward in their business?

STEPHEN: I think understanding who it is you want to communicate with is most important. Especially when you're coming from a marketing perspective, everybody evolves around their GAPs. GAP is an acronym for Goals, Actions (or Activities), and Priorities.

Everybody has this big thing they want to become or do or experience, and they set these goals that they look to achieve. They may be micro-goals that help them to hit the macro-goal, and there are all these different activities or actions that are taken to reach those goals. Then there is a way that they go about prioritizing their resources, like how they prioritize their time, how they prioritize their money, etc.

I think having an understanding of that small element of the world is important in looking at how we can respectfully communicate with them.

The worst thing you can do is compete against somebody's priorities. That means, if you're trying to communicate a message to somebody that's not meaningful to them, there's no relevancy there to them, then chances are, you're going to have a very, very difficult time getting them to even listen to you.
If we start from a community level, understanding that these groups of people self-organize around things that are most important to them, rather than things that piss them off,

Why Can't We Say What We Mean?

or those things that they're passionate about, good or bad, or things that they're excited about, they self-organize around these things.

If you become part of a community and you understand the language that they use and need to become a part of the conversations that are taking place, it will become much, much easier to have those levels of interactive communication that we're looking for to facilitate business transactions; like joint ventures, affiliate recruitment, selling of more products to more individuals and even more products to single individuals, and just ultimately grow the value that we have of the marketplace, surely, because we have a better understanding of what's going on in the minds of our market and what the priorities are.

JED: Yeah. That just brings me to the next question. And that's how you're doing this, that's exactly how you're doing this.

I know that you're really big with this Web 2.0 and building relationships there. You have active accounts on Facebook, MySpace,

Yuie. Why do you feel that it's so important to connect with people in social marketing, social networking situations?

STEPHEN: Because that's where the people are. The times are changing. This world has evolved significantly over a short period of time. We can't be stuck in one world saying, "This is the way I'm going to do it, because this is the way that I've always done it."

The world is changing. I think not using these channels is kind of like saying you don't need a cell phone, or you're still using a rotary phone of some kind. I don't even think that the telecom companies can even support a rotary phone, for the most part anymore.

The point is that this old school, this old technology is slower. Where we live today, the environment that we live in today that is really technology and Internet driven, things are constantly changing fast.

Remember, this whole thing about technology is not about the technology itself. It's not necessarily about MySpace itself, or Yuie itself, or Facebook itself, or LinkedIn itself, or Squidoo itself, or Twitter itself.

Why Can't We Say What We Mean?

It's really about the people that are congregating in those particular places.

Really, it's just marketing. You go where the money is. If you want to go where the money is, you have to go where the market is. The market is congregating. They're building communities over there, and that's where it is you need to be. If that's where they're holding the conversations, then that's where it is you need to be. If that's where the highest level of interaction is taking place, then that's where you need to be.

JED: Isn't that the truth? We're seeing such massive growth in that Web 2.0 technology so quickly, products and services alone, not to mention all of the connection points.

As far as a teacher, trainer, mentor, and what I like to call a "human change agent," you have a very, very powerful influence on those of us that you come in contact with. What do you do to maintain your vision, your direction, your thirst, and your desire to keep on connecting with us?

www.jedthecommunicator.com

STEPHEN: One thing is I understand why it is I do what it is that I do. I think it's important for all of us to really get in touch with why it is we do what we do.

What is the mission? What is the vision? What's the purpose? What's the meaning? What's the motivation? What is that thing that has that fire burning in our gut, that thing that makes our heart beat faster, the reason we're getting up earlier in the morning and going to bed a little bit later at night and we're not tired or exhausted but still energized? Even in moments of fatigue, we still feel more alive than at any other point and time in our life.

That's getting in touch with ultimately what this thing means. When the money is gone or it's not the biggest issue, and there are all these nice things you can accumulate materially, what is that remaining thing when you strip all of that away?

For me, it's always been about creating new possibilities for myself and for others. There's nothing more that I could think of that lights me up than seeing somebody that really gets it. They understand that we live

Why Can't We Say What We Mean?

in a time and place right now that the possibilities are endless.

We've always known that we have infinite potential and there's infinite wealth in this world. But I don't think there's ever been a time like today where it's been more demonstrated that we have infinite potential, and that's there's infinite work in the time that we live in today.

When I see people, they take advantage of that and their life just becomes completely transformed, not just financially, but in all of the areas of their life, emotionally, in their relationships, and stuff. There's just something about that.

I understand that. That's why it is I do this. That's what it is I'm going for. That's why I'm even talking to you right now.

Get in touch with why it is you do what you do; what's the meaning behind every action, behind every email, behind every call, behind every sentence that you put a dot or an explanation mark behind.

www.jedthecommunicator.com

What's the motivation, ultimately, the ultimate reason why you get up in the morning and you feel as if you are here to serve a certain group of people, provide a significant amount of value and, in return, be rewarded financially.

Basically, it's understanding why it is that I'm here, why it is I do what it is I do that really, really keeps me going.

JED: I don't know what to say. Offline before we started, I told you and I'm going to publicly acknowledge you. That is exactly why I'm here right now, because of you and your wife and what you've done for me and my family to help direct and guide and teach. The light finally came on. Stephen, again, thank you very, very much.

STEPHEN: You're welcome.

JED: That brings me to the last component of this interview is to talk a little bit about what specifically you're doing. I hear you are communicating with your market and giving away a lot of free content. That's www.dtalpha.com/talkback. That's a new audio blog and podcasting, which is awesome.

Why Can't We Say What We Mean?

I've been there on Mondays and it's great. I thoroughly enjoy the content, the no fluff. Do you think by talking to your audience in these audio blogs, you're able to communicate and reach them better?

STEPHEN: Yes. It's really creating, capturing them and cultivating and nurturing and fostering relationships. It's a thing where I know that there's a fine line between creating scarcity for your appearance by not making yourself too available to people, but at the same time being more available, where you create a certain bond and relationship with people.

You have to strike that medium. If you think about how often people see Oprah and the connection that she creates with people, like five days a week. In fact, it's even more than that now. Larry King and Ellen DeGeneres; it's really about understanding that people love to have conversations, and at a minimum, they love to listen to conversations that are intriguing and relevant to them. They're able to live through other people's lives and take in other people's experiences and perspectives and learn from those, or

Copyright © 2008. Jed A. Reay. All rights reserved.

at a minimum, they find some form of entertainment in those that makes them feel good.

What it is that I'm doing is something that's pretty much part of our history, part of who we are and something that we're just engineered to look for and to accept. And that is human interaction with other people; the nature of conversations, listening to them and participating in them, because that's how we live and that's how we go through this world. No man is an island unto himself.

My self-serving ended a long time ago. I used to give stuff away for free. I know some people who said, "Oh, my God! Don't give away your stuff for free. You should charge people for it."

We have a ton of stuff that we do charge for and that we will continue to charge for, and new stuff that we'll be coming out with. But I don't think that people consider what it is you're sharing with them to be a no-value just because you're getting it for free.

That's just like saying that the kind of people that are able to watch a certain show on television for free,

Why Can't We Say What We Mean?

they're not paying for it with cable or some part of free cable or something, that they don't enjoy the show, that it's not valuable for them, and that it's not a part of their life.

I don't believe that to be true. I believe that when you make a certain level of connection with people and that they've developed a certain relationship with you, where now it is more beyond you and them, but it's us, they think of it in terms of being us.

It's really about pushing it to the point where you get the right answer to the question of, "If you stop doing what you're doing, would you be missed?"

If the answer to that is no, then there's a problem. If the answer to that is yes, then maybe you have created the kind of relationships in your market that are meaningful enough, that will reward you with the kind of financial increase that it is you would look for with maybe membership sites, continuity programs, coaching programs, or one-up products or events, or whatever it is you're looking to do.

www.jedthecommunicator.com

I think at the very base of it, the thing that really fuels the entire thing is that it's trying a relation of a community, the conversation, and the interaction.

JED: That rings with me. That really does. You're giving away a free book to people. Why are you doing that?

STEPHEN: We wrote a book that we're giving away. It's a 133-page book called *Make More Money On The Internet.* It's really to provide the kind of valuable insights for people that show them that, for one, making money on the Internet is simple. Although it's simple, there is a process to it.

Our whole thing is to demonstrate and show and articulate for people that "This is what it really comes down to and these are the elements that are involved." As a result of this, we hope to build relationships with people on a deeper level and a different level that puts them in a position where they're like, "You know what? I'm going to continue to move forward with you."

And they end up investing in other programs that are valuable to them and that help them to reach those goals, to properly do those activities

Why Can't We Say What We Mean?

and take the right kinds of actions, and also to help them to better improve or perform those things that they consider to be a priority and, ultimately, reach what it is they want to reach.

Whether you want to sell automobiles, real estate, direct sales, network marketing, physical goods, digital goods, it doesn't matter. The Internet is just this amazing, amazing channel that allows people of younger ages more than at any time before now, and older ages with very little resources, regardless of how many resources you have, you can start with little resources and amass a fortune, if that's what you want to do.

If you want part-time income, full-time income, or you want to become just drunk with wealth, the Internet allows us to do it.

The purpose of the free book that we give away is to show people the fundamentals. At the end of the day, you have to measure the fundamentals of anything, whether it's sports or business. You have to measure the fundamentals, even in life. What are the fundamentals of

www.jedthecommunicator.com

just walking, talking? If you don't have the certain fundamentals in place, it becomes nearly impossible to participate in the game, not to mention try to win the game.

Our whole purpose of this book is to introduce them to the fundamentals that they can use immediately and get some kind of results from. Hopefully, because of the way that we've given it to them, they open up to us and feel like this is a relationship that they want to pursue on a higher, yet deeper level, that opens up to further exchanges of value.

JED: Wow! Where can they get access to this free book?

STEPHEN: They can go to www.makerealmoneyontheinternet.com and the book is $19.95. However, it is a physical book and all they have to do is pay the shipping. If they're in the United States, that's less than $5. It's a beautifully designed, very easy to read book, 133 pages.

The feedback that we've been getting on this is absolutely amazing. There are people who would have paid a ton of money for this. This

Why Can't We Say What We Mean?

free book is better than things that they paid for and they got in thousands of dollars of courses.

The reason why is because I really consider myself to be the kind of guy that likes to strip away the fat, strip away the fluff, strip away the filler and just give people the meat, not giving something like 500 pages or 10 audios that can be said in 133 pages.

It's stated in such a way that people can get it. I really believe the truth of understanding something on a mastery level is when you can take something that's difficult and explain it to people in very few words and they're able to get it. That's the way that I view it.

They can go to www.makerealmoneyontheinternet.com and they can claim their copy of the book and we'll rush it right to their door. It's a physical book and it's amazing. They don't have to pay the regular price of $19.95. All we do ask is that they cover the small shipping fee for us to get that out to their door. They'll get it in a few days and they'll love it. I promise you.

Copyright © 2008. Jed A. Reay. All rights reserved.

www.jedthecommunicator.com

JED: I can attest to anything that Stephen puts on or provides. I'm a past coaching client, and what I'm doing here is all because of Stephen Pierce and his organization. So I can speak directly to this.

Stephen, I can't begin to thank you for the time that you've given us. This project is almost coming to completion now and it's quite exciting.

You can find Stephen on www.dtalphal.com/talkback and you can also find him on www.stephenworldtour.com.

Stephen Pierce, thank you so very much for your time.

STEPHEN: Thank you, I appreciate you having me. What you're doing is an amazing thing, and I really do hope that it reaches thousands and thousands of people and changes thousands and thousands of lives. Congratulations to you and everybody involved.

JED: Thank you.

STEPHEN: Thank you.

Copyright © 2008. Jed A. Reay. All rights reserved.

Why Can't We Say What We Mean?

CHAPTER 12:
INTERVIEW WITH
STEVEN SADLEIR

Mr. Steven Sadleir

Steven Sadleir is Director and co-founder of the **Self Awareness Institute**, founded in 1985, and recognized as a **Shaktipat Master** in two lineages. A scholar and lecturer of philosophy, he has studied meditation with many of the world's enlightened masters to complete his training as a yogi.

Steven has developed powerful distance learning programs for people of all cultures and faiths and welcomes those who are ready for full self-realization. He has trained thousands of people from over 120 counties to meditate and find greater clarity, happiness and peace, and reaches many through his Enlightenment Radio meditative programs heard at

www.live365.com/stations/sair?site=pro

www.jedthecommunicator.com

His books include *Looking for God, A Seeker's Guide to Religious and Spiritual Groups of the World*, and his most recent, *Self Realization, An Owner-User Manual for Human Beings*. With his amazing communication skills and brilliant abilities to connect the human spirit, Steven is a true asset to the human consciousness.

For more information about Steven's **distance learning programs** and FREE Guided Meditation MP3s visit www.selfawareness.com

INTERVIEW

JED: Good afternoon, everyone. This is Jed Reay, "The Communicator." I'm coming to you from sunny, beautiful Northwest Oregon, and I have a very special guest on the line for all of you joining me today.

I would like to introduce Steven Sadleir, the Director of Self-Awareness Institute, the voice of Enlightened Radio heard in 120 countries, and bestselling author of *Looking for God*. Steven Sadleir, welcome.

STEVEN: Thank you, it's great to be here.

JED: You and I have a special relationship, and I do have to say that

Why Can't We Say What We Mean?

I'm blessed to know you. I can only say that all those that don't know you yet, they will someday soon, I've got to say.

Basically, what we're doing here is having a conversation about communication, and you have a very unique way of communicating with the world. I found that listening to your meditations and being involved in your meditations and being involved in your program has changed my life already. I look for great things to happen.

The reason that I asked for you to be involved in this project was because of the way that you communicate to us. I'd kind of like to start out with just a couple of questions and get a dialogue going.

What does it mean to communicate and develop meaningful relationships in a business arena?

STEVEN: It's interesting. That's a great question, because there are so many depths, or layers, to communication for me. On the one end, there's the intellectual, the mental taking in of data information through your ears or through your eyes and assimilating it. You have your own cognitive processes where you'll relate to each word, and your mind will come up with different meanings to the words and sentences that you're communicating, depending on what your life experience is.

But there's a whole other level in the level of the emotion, the heart, and how you're connecting. How do you connect with another person? The medium can make a big difference in that.

I would argue that there is even a third level, if not more, and that's at the level of the spirit. In all our communications, whether it's through the telephone, through our teleconference courses, or through Internet, so many of the things that we share and express are in a digital format, so an email, say.

Yet, a whole other realm, which is kind of new, is through the Shaktipat, or the transmission of energy; pure communication of spirit to spirit, which deliberately bypasses the mental filters and the emotional responses and takes you into a level of communication that most people aren't even conscious of.

Why Can't We Say What We Mean?

There's almost a matrix of communication, and some people use part of the matrix, some use others. What we're trying to do is integrate them so that we can be communicating at many different levels.

JED: I agree with you. I can actually say with all confidence that I'm aware of that. I always used to communicate with my little monkey, I called it, of the subconscious mind, but I wasn't fully aware of the power that it actually had until I met you.

It has allowed me to grow as a person, as a husband, as a father, and as a business partner, business person, as someone that works with many different people from all across the world. I have to give you some credit for my success, Steven, thank you very much.

In your opinion, what characteristics or abilities, assuming that they're not innate, does one need to be an effective communicator?

STEVEN: I think the main one is the desire to communicate. Again, some people communicate at a kind of a mental level, an intellectual level. It's a process-oriented information flow. Some people are more impassive, in that what they really are looking for or needing, either in their expression or in their listening, is a heart connection.

What we're finding, and what you found through the course, is that there's yet another level that most people are kind of oblivious to, or only dimly aware of, which is the level of communicating spirit to spirit and soul to soul. I think that's one of the greatest needs in the human experience that has been overlooked.

You can't as effectively communicate at that level without those other levels too. So I think it's kind of like the idea of bringing body, mind and spirit all together so that they're aligned, and each can support the other in almost a synergistic way, if you use it effectively.

JED: It seems that when I come in contact with new clients or potential partners in my business, I run up against some difficulties. There is this perception that communication is difficult, that I don't know what to

Why Can't We Say What We Mean?

say and I don't know how to say it. I bring that back to I always have this quite comical way of lightening this conversation and to not be stressful about having a conversation with anyone. I always like to say, "Are you married?" and hopefully they say yes, because if they say no, then my whole point doesn't work.

If they say yes, I say, "You didn't have a conversation with your wife or your husband about marrying you? You did sell them, you did promote yourself, you did communicate a desire and a message."

Ultimately, that is what I hope happens, when we interact back and forth with people, is that we're looking to this other person.

A good way to say it is, "What is it that I can do to help you in your life? Is there anything that I could be or say or do to support you?" And that opens up this floodgate of communication, of interactions, of sharing.

With that being said, can you give our audience maybe some simple steps to improve their ability to connect and communicate with someone?

STEVEN: Yes. I think one is a clear communication of your intention in your communication. I like to use this, "This is my intention for being with you, Jed, is to help you," and so forth, or "to help the audience learn to communicate better."

You give someone the clarity of why you're communicating, because a lot of times it may be implicit and not always understood by the person that's listening to you.

We live in a world where people are always trying to sell us something or have other. maybe "ulterior" motives. Being clear on what the intent of the communication is can be disarming, and it can allow a certain amount of vulnerability, too.

If you're letting someone know you're coming from the heart and your intention is to help them communicate better, then they may not jump to the conclusion that you're making them wrong, if they bring up something that they're sensitive about, as an example.

Why Can't We Say What We Mean?

The other thing that I think is an effective communication tool is to ask questions and to say, "Well look, how are you hearing me? What did you hear me say? I want to make sure I'm communicating well and that it's feeling good for you, not just that the information is being heard."

If you put it that way, it might sound like you're talking down to them, and they'll say, "Of course, I understood what you said. I heard every word. I know the English language."

But what you're really saying, and if you make it clear that this is what you mean is, "I want to make sure that I'm communicating well with you, Jed, in this instance."

I say, "What do you hear me saying? How are you hearing what I'm saying?" In doing so, you can allow someone to be more open in expressing, because maybe they've heard a word you used and you didn't mean it in the context in which they heard it, as an example.

Then you say, "Oh, thank you for sharing. Let me clarify what I meant by that, because I really didn't mean it to come off that way."

We were talking about emails. That's an example, because sometimes in an email you can say something and somebody might read something into the email that you didn't intend, pro or con. Asking the question helps create that clarity in the communication.

I think expressing what your intention is in the communication is one thing, asking a question is the other.

I like to use another realm, because those are both intellectual processes. I like to say, "How do you feel? Do you feel good about what we talked about?" Again, it's usually a question, but it's taking it out of the realm of the mind.

So many people process things mentally. And incidentally, studies have been done with women, and both men and women process emotionally too, but women are predominantly empathic in their communication. If you ask someone how they feel, it takes it out of the realm of just words and understanding, but it helps people

Why Can't We Say What We Mean?

relate at a deeper level. It allows them to be a little more vulnerable and open. It provides for a deeper level of communication.

JED: That reminds me of something many, many, many years ago as a young child. I would always say, "You did," or "you said."

It was interesting because he asked me, "When you say something like that, it makes me feel as though I'm either not doing right by you, or you're misunderstanding what I'm doing. Could you explain what you mean by saying to me that this is how I feel when you do this?"

It was very enlightening for me as a young person, because it did change the whole dynamics. It changed the whole chemistry within my body about what I was communicating. I learned that real early as a child. Sometimes I still forget it, but it's a very powerful point about how we feel.

I look at your ability to connect with people in a far greater way than what is normally done on a person-to-person basis; those communication skills, your ability at a level far from the norm.

What would you suggest we do in this area of consciousness to become more enlightened? Obviously, you provide a service, many services, a radio show, the Self-Awareness Institute. Can you talk to us a little bit about what you do for the world?

STEVEN: Sure. I'll approach that with the question you started, "What can we do to become more enlightened?"

I think it's really understanding that there's an intention to be enlightened, you see, because a lot of people don't look at their life in terms of there being an enlightenment for an awakening of consciousness, or an evolution of consciousness.
There are so many words to describe something that's intuitive to everybody, and that is this desire to evolve ourselves to learn and grow to what Maslow would call "self-actualized," and yogis have called "self-realized."

This sense of enlightenment is used rather broadly, but it all really kind of connotes that there is a deeper level of awareness and something to

Why Can't We Say What We Mean?

connect with, and there's the potential that we have to live in a state where there is more happiness and peace, yet it's not always talked about.

Some people actually feel a little off put, frightened, or uncomfortable with the idea that there is an enlightenment. Once you've realized that there's something to be realized, then your realization has begun. Once you've acknowledged in your mind that there is an enlightenment, there is a higher state of consciousness that you can attain.

If it's clear in your mind and you see that as an intention in your life, all of a sudden, your life shifts in a dramatic way. You will start looking at things you can do to improve yourself.

Once you've gained that clarity in your mind, that opens up pathways for whatever it is you need to come to you, like that ancient saying, "When the student is ready, the teacher appears." And so, I appear, maybe because you're listening to this program, or listening to this interview.

www.jedthecommunicator.com

When you say, "What can people do?" the first step is to recognize that you're seeking, and that which you are seeking is causing you to seek. There is something inside you that is kind of compelling you, creating a sense of curiosity, a drive to develop yourself.

Now, anybody can come to our website at www.selfawareness.com and they can download a free MP3 guided meditation, or talks that I've done on the radio. You can get information where you can kind of sample it in a way that's convenient, it's free and it's accessible to everyone, and kind of scout around and see how it feels.

There's going to be an intellectual process and there's going to be an emotional process, but ultimately your spirit is going to guide you wherever you need to be.

The next step would be maybe something a little more proactive, such as getting on a free call. I do a free call every month. As a matter of fact, I do three this month. I do a free meditation, because my book was on world religions and I'm developing a course that can be done online, so I'm recording. This month I'm

Why Can't We Say What We Mean?

talking about Buddhism and Daoism. Last week, I talked about Hinduism and Yoga, so I'm kind of going through these different categories of teachings.

It's a way that people can kind of plug in, and any discussions of the spiritual nature, wherever your inclination leads you, starts to foster not only that curiosity that kind of creates a momentum for your development, but more importantly, it sparks a connection with the part of you that already knows, because the answers lie within you.

The real goal isn't to try and just inform somebody or give a technique, but to engage that inner knowledge, to connect with that part of you that already knows who you are and why you were born, so you can fulfill the purpose of your existence. That's how you find fulfillment and meaning and peace in your life, is by connecting with that inner knowing and being aligned with your purpose and destiny.

JED: I can say with all the confidence in the world that being involved with The Institute, being involved with you and sharing with other students has been literally the most exhilarating thing that I've ever done in my life. I am truly blessed.

I will close with this final question. I think that part of me already knows the answer, but it's important, because people like yourself are so busy. I mean, we're in so much contact.

Let's be honest. You are on the run all the time, and the one thing as a teacher, trainer, mentor, human change agent, a power of influence on those of us that you come in contact with is great. What do you do to maintain your vision, your direction, your thirst, your hunger, and your desire to continue connecting like you do?

STEVEN: The key is in me, realizing that I don't really do anything. The key is in realizing that there is a power greater than me that makes my own heart beat, and I just give myself over to that.

I literally have a prayer, "Lord, how may I serve thee?" I don't think in terms of what I want or what needs to be done. As long as I'm connected with that, it's my source of

Why Can't We Say What We Mean?

inspiration and self, because it is spirit itself.

What I am is spirit. This is what you are, is innately spirit. When our spirit is gone, we're dead, right? That what animates us is us. And so, if you're living in the awareness of the spirit that you are, there's nothing but inspiration. It's your spirit in expression without the encumbrance, or, at least, a minimal encumbrance of the mind and body with its own ideas that may differ from what's in your highest and best good.
The more you allow your spirit to guide you, the more you live spirited. There's a constant state of inspiration, because that's your true nature.

JED: I knew what your answer was going to be, but it really, truly seems to be the common theme of everyone that I have interviewed for this project, is that it's not them.

Their inspiration, their power, their influence, everything that they do is centered around the spirit that keeps them focused, keeps them going straightforward. And all the more reason, because there are a lot of tools out there that we have yet to communicate with.

With that being said, Steven Sadleir, thank you so very much. I know for a fact that our audience is going to enjoy this very much, and I look forward to our relationship into the future.

STEVEN: Thank you for having me on. I look forward to meeting your audience again.

JED: Yeah, brother, we're blessed.

STEVEN: God bless you.

Why Can't We Say What We Mean?

CHAPTER 13: INTERVIEW WITH JOEL THERIEN

Mr. Joel Therien

Joel Therien is a well-known, successful Internet MLM marketer who has accumulated hundreds of thousands of affiliates selling his products and services in the past 10 years. He has created an amazing **systemized residual income model** that he teaches others how to duplicate.

Joel was one of the very first pioneers who used the affiliate MLM direct sales offline model and the power of the Internet to change direct sales marketing forever. His companies are among the double-digit million revenue earners. His numbers are impressive, and he writes checks in the tens of thousands every month to his affiliates, paying well over $1 million in commissions monthly.

President of hotconference.com and Kiosk.ws Joel has also launched www.opportunitymarketplace.com which enables people to communicate for free using real-time audio and video conferencing.

Contact Joel at www.hotconference.com for information on how to maximize your online communication needs, and be sure to ask about his **MLM residual income model.**

INTERVIEW

JED: Good morning, everyone. This is Jed Reay. I'm coming to you with a fabulous, fabulous interview. I have the honored privilege to speak with Joel Therien.

Joel is the president of www.wwkiosk.com and www.kiosk.ws and www.hotconference.com and www.opportunitymeetingplace.com. Joel comes to us with an extensive, extensive background within the communication network of using the Internet.

We started off this project with a mindset heading down a certain path. I have been turned around almost 180 degrees to back to center. It's because of people like Joel that provide us a mechanism for actually providing healthy, meaningful communication on the Internet.

Why Can't We Say What We Mean?

Joel, welcome.

JOEL: Thank you very much, Jed. It's a pleasure to be here. It's a real honor.

JED: Let me start by asking you just a couple of questions that can start us on this personal communication path here in this interview, like if someone were to ask you, "Joel, what does it mean to communicate and develop meaningful relationships in a business arena?"

JOEL: One of the aspects that I see on the Internet that a lot of people make mistakes around, and so forth, it really depends on whether it's one-on-one communication or one-to-many communication. The Internet is a very effective tool at generating communication for both.

One of the things that I want to touch upon, that I even learned before jumping on the Internet, was actually taught to me by my father. It centers around communications.

The one thing that I've always done is make sure, first and foremost, you become a good listener. By listening to the needs and the marketplace out there, you ultimately become a good

www.jedthecommunicator.com

communicator. I see so many people talking about this and that and really not listening, first and foremost.

The old saying is, "That's why you have two ears and one mouth, you should be listening double the amount of time that you should actually be talking." That's really how I became an effective communicator online, by listening to what's out there, by reading forums, reading the communication of others, reading other people's blogs, and so forth.

That's why email is great for one-to-one communications with people that you have an established relationship with.

What a lot of your audience will find is as their business grows online, email becomes very ineffective for communications. If you start, and you're probably in the same place, Jed, getting 400, 500, 600 emails a day, it's literally impossible.

In fact, you and I almost missed each other because of that exact fact. You're getting so many emails and I'm getting so many emails. Of course, there are SPAM traps out there and everything else in between.

Why Can't We Say What We Mean?

It's still a great medium, email, but it's not a good medium for conversation with many. I think that's why blogging and MySpace and all the others have become so popular.

JED: Isn't that interesting? I agree. We did trade emails there back and forth, or, at least, I was sending emails and they were getting missed just because of the threshold. What is it that you put into the subject line in order for someone that you don't know or doesn't know you that would be open enough to open that email? Chances are it takes some prodding from a third party to at least get that to happen.

Isn't that interesting? Initially, my comment was that there is this faceless, nameless mechanism on the Internet. We have to take great consideration and great thought and interest in order to develop healthy communication using this medium. I agree with you.

Let me ask you this. Assuming that being able to communicate, and you said you learned this from your father, that listening was a critical characteristic and component of communication, assuming it's not innate, what kind of characteristics or abilities does one need to be an effective communicator in the business world?

JOEL: I think coming back to that point. One, you really have to get rid of the distractions, if you want to be a good communicator in business. We definitely live in an attention-deficit world. Email is just one medium that people can get us at. Now there are cell phones, there's text messaging, there are your home phones, and there's the aspect of many people who are jumping online raising a family.

I think one of the best ways to being a good communicator, and this is probably going to sound silly, but what I do is I definitely meditate on a daily basis to find out what is the most important aspect of my communications for the day. What is going to best allocate my time to communicate effectively with certain people in the marketplace that are going to generate a strong leverage point for me?

That's something that I definitely recommend. If you want to be a good communicator in the business world, definitely eliminate as many distractions in your life as you can.

Why Can't We Say What We Mean?

Turn off the cell phone for a couple of hours a day. Read your emails attentively for the people that you want to communicate with, and definitely align yourself with other great communicators across the Internet world.

A lot of our clients come to us and say, "How do I start hanging with the bigwigs?" I think it's just being an effective communicator. Whether you want to call it a click or a niche of individuals, it's really centered around that, eliminating distractions on a daily basis.

For example, you and I finally hooked up because I took one of my days and I said, "Okay, I need to go through my emails here and find out what's important, what's not important."

Evidently, that's how we finally found each other. I found your email. I emailed you back and said, "I apologize, Jed. I've been really busy with things that are very distracting in my life right now. We're building a new data center in San Antonio."

That is definitely one of the ways of becoming an effective communicator, eliminating distractions, so that you can communicate effectively to your marketplace.

JED: Right.

JOEL: Absolutely.

JED: It really is very, very true. The more that we expose ourselves, the more that you and I grow as individuals, as businesses, our companies and our exposure grows using this medium also, so does the distraction grow.

I agree with you wholeheartedly. That is a critical component. It's amazing. Most of the very, very successful entrepreneurs today, it appears that they're all saying the same thing.

I have to pick the time, number one, a very short period of time every day that I mess around with emails. But I only respond to those that, like you said, that trigger some kind of demand on my time or response from my time, or for that matter, a relationship that's going to leverage my efforts and my time and also leverage my income.

It's interesting that everybody has made that comment. That being said,

Why Can't We Say What We Mean?

can you give our audience some insight of where they might go, either offline or online, where they might go to get some help and some guidance and some direction from your perspective and your experience to help them with the communication?

JOEL: I think definitely they need to know the fundamentals. If they're going to be communicating via the Internet, of course, the first and foremost thing that pops up is you need to know the fundamentals.

You don't need to be an expert, but you need to know the fundamentals. You need to know how to get a website up. You definitely need to know how to put a blog online, because that's the core of the communication.

As an example, people should register their names as the domain name. I own the domain names of myself and all my kids, Livia Therien, Justin Therien, because I know that that will one day, and it probably already is, be the center of communication. Get yourself out there. In essence, get noticed by other people and become an effective communicator that way.

www.jedthecommunicator.com

If the people want to communicate via the Internet, they need to know the fundamentals. I think that's where a lot of the hype in the Internet comes around. You don't need to know anything. You don't need to know HTML. You don't need to know web design. You don't need to know what a domain name is.

I personally think that's a bunch of BS, if you will. You don't need to be an expert. Do I know how to design a beautiful website? No. Do I know how to upload my picture on my blog?

Essentially, what I use for effective communication is I do video blogs all the time on www.joeltherien.com. It's the most effective belly-to-belly communication that I can have to the masses that makes it as personable as it can be.

Knowing the fundamentals is definitely important. I hope you would agree. You see so much hype on the net about "You don't need to know anything. It's a click of a mouse and you're done and you're going to make $10,000."

Why Can't We Say What We Mean?

JED: Right.

JOEL: That's essentially not true. You need to put yourself out there. I remember when I first got started online, I would come up with a great idea at 11:30 at night. I had hired a web designer in the interim while I was trying to learn this stuff. Of course, you can't call a guy at midnight or 1:00 in the morning to share your inspiration. You're paying them $10 an hour to design your web page for you.

JED: Oh, come on. Why not?

JOEL: You know what I mean? Knowing the fundamentals is definitely going to help people out.

JED: Sure.

JOEL: Where can you go to learn those fundamentals? There are all types of free resources online. Google is an amazing resource that I still use. You just go and Google the keywords that you're looking for. You'll find some great information on the aspects of the fundamentals.

The other thing, because we're talking about attention deficit, other people who want to have effective communications online, and this goes against the grain of the Internet, but it's an integral part that's very important. My business almost tripled in size. I'm one of the old folks, where I really bought into the whole aspect of work from home and stuff, and I do. I work 99% of my day from home. But still, nothing beats the belly-to-belly communication.

JED: Right.

JOEL: Get to some local or nation-based Internet marketing seminars.

JED: Yes.

JOEL: Go and meet and network with some of the people, develop a relationship with people. To a certain extent, using effective mass communications like video and audio and Facebook and MySpace, and all that kind of stuff will help build your communication medium, but you still need to do some traveling.

A lot of people on this call might say, "I don't have the budget for it."

I would say invest in your education. You're going to need to spend some aspect of your current income in

Why Can't We Say What We Mean?

getting to some of these events. It's very important.

I had already been online for seven years, I believe, and the first event that I went to was the Internet Marketing Main Event. It was one of Mike Filsaime's events. I really didn't want to go. I'm very much a homebody.

JED: Right.

JOEL: I wanted to spend time with my family and my kids, and I didn't want to travel. He kept bugging me and bugging me and bugging me, and I went and it was just a huge aha moment for me.

We started picking up all types of big clients, people like Mike Filsaime, Mark Joyner, Armand Morin, people like yourself and others who started using our hosting services. Not because I was an effective communicator online, but because of just communicating with them person-to-person, establishing a friendship and a relationship, using that relationship for effective communications down the road.

JED: Right.

JOEL: That's important as well. It goes a little bit against the grain of communications via the Internet, but it still is a small percentage of importance. Like when you meet people, that's important as well.

JED: I do have to tell you that I agree wholeheartedly with you. My history is belly-to-belly, continually built for businesses, all with my feet, and know that now I'm not interested in wearing out my feet anymore.

I'm going to take that knowledge and bring it to the Internet and have both. I agree with you wholeheartedly that education and that face-to-face interaction is critical. That just brings us right to this point.

You've got one that you're going to be involved in this week. You know?

JOEL: Yeah.

JED: There's a great conference that's starting this week. If I remember correctly, that's an annual conference, something that's on an international basis. There are people from all over the world that will attend. You want to speak to that a little bit?

Why Can't We Say What We Mean?

JOEL: Absolutely. I'll be speaking at that World Internet Summit in Dallas on May 22. It comes back to something that might be very intriguing. First, I want to take one step back. For those of you in the audience you might say, "I really don't want to travel."

Listen, it's a very small percentage. The Internet is very effective, but it's just a necessary component. If you travel once a year, once every couple of years, if you've never been to an event, try to at least make it to one. You'll see the value there very quickly.

A lot of people say, "Look, I can't afford the hotel. I can't afford the travel. I can't afford the time away from the home." I guarantee if you get to one of these events, you'll see that there's huge value there.

What landed me this speaking gig, and this is being quite honest with people, because you and I were speaking before this call, Jed, that I was really an individual who definitely branded my company names first, which is www.kiosk.ws and www.hotconference.com, and then branded my name maybe a little bit more after that.

www.jedthecommunicator.com

What landed me this gig was one of the most effective communication mediums out there right now, blogging. I do a video blog twice a week. I try to do it every Monday and Friday, giving people some great advice, and very often it's just updates on what I'm doing.

Here's a key to communication. The more you can let people into your personal life in a mass communication that way, what I mean by that is if people go to www.joeltherien.com and surf a lot of my video blogs, there are videos about my kids on there. There're videos about the new data center we're building. There're videos about my wife and I. The more that you can let people into your world and establish a relationship with them, the more in tune they're going to be to listen to your blog further down the road.

JED: Right.

JOEL: What you'll find is I have a very interactive blog. The reason why blogging is working is it's effective communication back and forth. There are a lot of different mediums out there.

Why Can't We Say What We Mean?

Websites are one-way communication. You're providing to your end client, or your perspective end client, off your website, the ad copy, so it's one-way communication. There's no real interaction.

The key to blogging that makes it so effective these days is people can create a dialog with you via your blog.

JED: Right.

JOEL: Of course, they can come and post back comments and you post back to them. It's two-way communication. I think that's why blogging has become so successful and so interesting to people.

Coming back to the point, my blog is so interactive with people it actually attracted the attention of Stephen and Tom and Brett McFall. They just emailed me and said, "Hey, Joel, you've got some great info on network marketing online and have a very interactive blog."

Obviously, what they did is they read between the lines and then said, "You must have a fairly large following of individuals in your company. Would you like to come and speak at our event?"

JED: Whoo-hoo!

JOEL: Just using that one communication medium, as I said earlier, getting yourself out there a little bit, understanding the fundamentals of how to put a blog up is what landed this gig for me.

JED: Right.

JOEL: That is just a mode of communication that has worked wonders.

A lot of other people, and I'll be one of the first persons to say that, before I started my blog it's like, "Why do I want to put something out there for free? Why do I want to allocate a certain amount of my day every day to go and put free blog posts out there? It's not really making me money."

Now I see the light, in that putting that out has definitely brought my name out there more and, in effect, has definitely generated a lot more income.

JED: Right.

Why Can't We Say What We Mean?

JOEL: A lot of the big Internet marketers have come and posted on my blog saying, "Hey, Joel, I like what you have to say about the infrastructure of your data center. I need servers. I need this. I need Hotconference. I need these tools."

By putting yourself out there, the money will come. It's the old adage, "If you build it, they'll come." And it's absolutely true.

JED: That speaks perfectly to exactly what this whole book and the series and the whole process is all about. The simple fact that when we provide value, truly, truly value on the front end, we are truly blessed on the back end from all of those that really do know who we are, what we want to do, and what our hopes and dreams and aspirations are.

It's interesting, because you can tell who's out on the front end trying to gain their upper hand with their hand up and out and wide open looking for cash on the front end, because they're not going to be successful long- term.

JOEL: No.

www.jedthecommunicator.com

JED: No one of any power or of influence is going to come to their aid and assist them. Isn't that the simple, simple process that has a running theme through all of this book and all the people that I've spoken with?

It is always value upfront first. Provide someone with service, provide someone with some content and information that helps them grow, whether it's personal or in their business.

Obviously, the whole premise here was business communication, but you also said something that I want to come to a conclusion with, which in a second I'll go back to. It is very powerful, and with one exception, everyone spoke to this.

Again, this issue of giving value upfront has opened many, many doors for you. It's already done the same for me. I'm just astonished at how many people came, just the door open wide, the flood gates of people coming to assist me with this process.

I knew nothing about writing a book. I've never written anything. I've got to tell you, I hated English and I wasn't very good at it.

Why Can't We Say What We Mean?

JOEL: Yeah, me too. Hey, we're on the same page there.

JED: This whole idea of videoing, Web 2.0 technology, and putting yourself out there, if you provide value to those listeners, they'll keep listening. And then, like you said, eventually somebody else in a position of influence of where you need to go is going to be there to help you along, because you're helping them.

JOEL: Absolutely. A good friend of mind, I don't know if you've ever watched A&E's "Flip This House" on TV, Armando Montelongo, I'll talk a little bit about that, if you like, is because I created value for Armando, which actually changed my whole career path. That's why I'm in San Antonio, Texas.

That's a totally different story. Even Stephen Pierce's tagline is "Create value to create wealth." I agree with you. I had no idea the type of doors that would open. It's the WIIFM radio station, right?

JED: Yep.

JOEL: What's in it for me radio.

JED: Yep.

JOEL: If you provide something to those people, it will come back hundreds, if not thousands of times back to you. You create a position for yourself of knowledge.

It's funny, a lot of people, and this is a stumbling block that I had to get over, is a lot of people who are new to the Internet might say, "I don't know anything. I don't have any expertise that I can provide of value to other people."

That is not true.

JED: Yes.

JOEL: Everybody, the Internet is so global that if you have any passion in your life, you've got knowledge that others want to hear about.

JED: Yep.

JOEL: There's no doubt about it. There's no doubt about it. Coming from a humble beginning, a lot of the top Internet marketers did come from a humble beginning. I still feel blessed today. I'm trying to search for the right words to say this.

Why Can't We Say What We Mean?

But even myself, I still think, "Why do people want to listen to me?"

Then you start to realize that, "The experience that I've built up over 12 years is common knowledge to myself." It's like I always say to myself, "People know that," and then you come to realize that no, they don't.

JED: No, they don't.

JOEL: This is knowledge that you've acquired over a long period of time that other people need. If you can help them skyrocket their success by not creating the same mistakes that you did, then you're going to create that value, which in the back end, as you said and I agree with you 1000% on, generates a whole lot of wealth.

JED: It's really quite amazing. Obviously, this book will give its credit where it's due. All of you have provided a great amount of insight for me. I didn't even come up with the idea. That was just it. My mastermind group came up with the idea. I just came up with the process and allowed the power of this entire system to do exactly what we're doing.

www.jedthecommunicator.com

Joel Therien would never have spoken with me, Jed Reay, from San Antonio to Eugene, Oregon. We would never have made a contact, first of all, if this idea had never come up. Even though I used the product, we probably would have never made a connection.

And that's exactly what Joel was just referring to with the type of connection that was made because of putting himself out there.

And I did the same thing, and lo and behold, here's this project. I have to tell you an aside, and then I want to close with a final question.

It was quite interesting. I had an aha experience when you talked about going to meetings and going around to do that face-to-face interaction and gain the education. It is critical that that happened. I might even say a little bit more.

Personally, I like being home. But at the same time, I might say maybe once a quarter, at least twice a year, go and be face-to-face with the people that are going to guide you.

This came up and it was really interesting. Just off the cuff, I made a

Why Can't We Say What We Mean?

comment to one of the interviewers the other day. I said, "The next book is going to be interviewing Oprah."

I got an email ten hours later from a very good friend in South Florida who said, "Rock and roll, baby. It's Oprah next," and it was not requested. There was nothing from it.

He says, "Oprah's next, 'Jed Reay, *New York Times* Bestseller.'"

And then I'm on the phone at the same time that email's coming with Gwen Fields, who is a movie producer in L.A. She lives in Beverly Hills. And I giggle and I'm reading this to her, and she goes, "When you're ready, let me know. I can get you inside the camp."

JOEL: Oh, Jed, six degrees of separation.

JED: That being said, let me ask you, and this is real powerful. You addressed it when you used the word meditation. I'm a very, very strong believer in some centralization of my body and spirit on a daily basis, twice a day at least. Sometimes I may need to do it more.

When you think about the energy that it takes to do what we do on a daily basis, day in and day out, and the interaction we have, the whole ADD scenario, that draws a lot of energy from us.

JOEL: Sure.

JED: What is it that you do to keep your tank full, so that you can provide value to the rest of the world?

JOEL: You're opening up a whole new can of worms. Here's the other thing that earned me a lot of respect. It's a complete side note. I used to be a professional athlete before I got online.

Needless to say, and I'm not tooting my horn, I'm in really great shape. I was a professional, natural bodybuilder. I'm 35 now, but I still stay in amazing, amazing shape. To answer your question specifically, I do train at least four times a week. I make the time, and I do mean that.

What I'll do on a training day to keep my energy, my battery going and my mind sharp is I will never, ever read one single email when I know it's gym day.

Why Can't We Say What We Mean?

I get up. This week I'm taking care of my kids, because my wife's gone back to Canada to visit some family. I'll get the kids off to school and it's to the gym right away. I know what happens if you start getting into your mode of communication for the day. The next thing you know, three hours have gone by and you're working away, and stuff like that.

I'm a big believer in healthy body, healthy mind.

JED: Yep.

JOEL: I watch what I eat on a daily basis. I take all my antioxidants, vitamins and minerals, and stuff like that. But what I was going to say is staying in top shape has earned me the respect with a lot of Internet marketers.

That's exactly how I landed a very large contract with Armando Montelongo from A&E's "Flip This House." We take care of his whole back end of his website, and he's generated millions of dollars online.

Here's an individual who gets thousands of emails a day, 4.2 million people watch his reality show every single week, and he gets thousands of fan emails every day.

He understands now why he answered my email, but he always thought, "This is a miracle. How did I pick your email out of a thousand emails a day that actually attracted my attention?"

If you want to land a bigwig out there, folks, we've been talking about this through our whole conversation here, Jed.

JED: Yep.

JOEL: All of us are extremely busy. We're always trying to find ways to recharge our batteries. We're meditating. We're doing a lot of things. My email was no more than one sentence long.

I get a lot of JV emails every day that are about two to three pages long.

JED: Yep.

JOEL: It usually starts, "Dear Mr. Therien, I don't want to take a lot of your time, but if you can read these three or six pages, then you'll see where I'm coming from."

Why Can't We Say What We Mean?

First and foremost, and I don't want this to sound pompous, but anybody who has time to write me a six-page email, I say to myself is somebody that's got too much time on their hands, which means their business is not built up yet.

JED: Yep.

JOEL: Obviously, there's no true leverage point there. It's not going to be a win-win. It's usually going to be, "Can you email your list of my brand new product, because I'm brand new to the Internet and I'll give you a commission on that." Well, that's not a true win-win.

The point being, I sent him about three words, if not three small sentences that said, "I can help you online. I'll fly down, come and see you."

That's how you land the bigwigs, folks. They're really busy individuals. Keep your emails very brief and offer something in it for them. Create value right away. That's how I did that.

As you can see, I have ADD myself, Jed, and I talked probably way too long on this one question. I just try to

	stay in shape. I train four times a week, it keeps me going.
JED:	I can't begin to thank you for the time that you've given to this project. Maybe there's something about this Internet thing, because I've always been and was actually medically diagnosed as ADD when I was a young child.
	I'm 51-years-old and I'm rewriting the script of my life. I'm having more fun than I've ever had in my life, and I get to communicate with some very, very, very interesting people, very caring and loving people. You yourself, right here is a great example of a great spirit.
	Joel Therien, I can't begin to thank you enough for the time that you've put in. I look forward to talking to you in real life.
JOEL:	Thank you so much, Jed. I feel very humbled taking part in this with you. It's a true blessing. I look forward to a really strong friendship and a relationship with you. Talking about that belly-to-belly, we're both belly-to-belly guys. Hopefully, we can hook up soon and go out and have lunch or something.

Why Can't We Say What We Mean?

JED: Sounds great.

JOEL: All right. Thanks so much, Jed. Take care.

JED: Thank you. Bye-bye.

Copyright © 2008. Jed A. Reay. All rights reserved

CONCLUSION

I sit here in awe of what has just taken place in my life in the past few months. Writing a book was the furthest thing from my mind, and when my mastermind group suggested it, I just about freaked. What I find so ironic about this whole process is that it is the *Law of Attraction* in full Technicolor.

I had been trying for a very long time to build a business online with little success. I started a journey and a quest for knowledge. I was doing a Wednesday morning motivational call for a group of business owners and at the same time reading an awesome book by Lynn Grabhorn, *Excuse Me, Your Life Is Waiting*.

This was very unusual for me to let go of control and just allow what I wanted to become a feeling, and focus on that feeling, and then allow. This all happened at the speed of light. I truly believe that what you put your visual attention on, focus with intensity, and then expect it to happen, THAT IT WILL.

I allowed my mastermind group to direct me because I was on uncharted waters, and the doors really just opened up wide. By making a commitment to the universe and a little help from my friends, the interviews just flowed. I am still amazed and truly honored at the involvement of those very successful 13 individuals. Each and every interview was very special to me, and I know they will be for you as well.

Why Can't We Say What We Mean?

This has been a very interesting process, one that I have decided to continue in the form of a series, *Why Can't We Say What We Mean?* Next, maybe communication in a personal relationship, or maybe a subset of more on business communication; stay tuned.

I did, however, find my initial position and opinion moved by doing these 13 interviews. I began this process with very colored glasses, almost blinder glasses about communication, technology, and how poorly we communicate. I still believe that in order to develop meaningful relationships, we must take an active role and truly participate in the process.

I can cite several situations of poor communication and what can happen as a result, but that would not solve the problem. We all are very capable of seeing the bad parts and focusing on what we do not want. What is going to move us forward as an interactive race is to focus on how to make our interactions positive, and focus on what we do want.

We have 13 very successful entrepreneurs, all from diverse backgrounds with varying perspectives, but yet all have very similar habits and rituals that attribute to their success. Let's discuss a few of the common themes, or attributes, that are inherent in these 13 interviews.

First, when communicating with another or a group, without exception, all of these interviewees indicated that providing value to the other person was critical. They all place a great sense of responsibility on providing true, measurable value

Copyright © 2008. Jed A. Reay. All rights reserved

to those they communicate with, whether they are customers, business associates, or contacts they make during their daily travels.

I am reminded of the way that Larry Benet makes a connection with someone new he has just met for the first time. I am paraphrasing. "Hello, Jed, what project are you currently working on right now that I could add value to and help you accomplish what you have set out to do?"

This is a great example of looking to add value to someone, instead of looking to see what you can get from them. This was a common theme in all the interviews. They all felt that by providing value to others first, that they would receive far more than if they had been focusing on their own needs first.

Secondly, it was obvious from these conversations that all 13 interviewees saw themselves as change agents. By using their gift and talents, they could be a beacon of hope to those they came in contact with. The results speak for themselves.

I challenge you to search each and every one of these successful people, look at their accomplishments, and you will find that they have been an inaugural part of helping to change the lives of those they work with.

Thirdly, all of these people carry with them a very healthy vision of self. They have a very strong and well-developed personal program of spiritual connection, which allows them to be good stewards of us all. They all are great teachers, mentors, or

Why Can't We Say What We Mean?

what I like to call change agents. They all use their gifts to be able to assist those they work with to move from a position of pain to a position of pleasure or success.

This whole process has truly been a pleasure for me. I hope that you have come away with new and enlightened insights as to how you can improve your life, improve your communication, by developing meaningful business relationships through effective communication.

I will leave you with this true story and some parting thoughts. I made an off-the-cuff remark to one of my mastermind members on the morning of May 12, 2008, "On the next project, I would be interviewing Oprah," and thought nothing of it.

At 8:12 p.m. PT that same day, I was on the phone with a friend and colleague, Gwen Fields, TV and movie producer from Hollywood. An email came in at the same time from a mutual friend of ours, John Barbar, Boca Raton, FL. John was responding to an earlier email and wrote, "Call me, man. I can see you on 'Oprah.' 'Mr. Jed *New York Times* Bestselling Author Reay.' Love you, brother."

Now, keep in mind that the earlier comment was not discussed with John, and I chuckled and shared this whole process with Gwen. She responded, "Better be careful with what you put forth to the universe, it will come to pass." She proceeded to say, "When you get ready, let me know and I'll get you in the front door."

Copyright © 2008. Jed A. Reay. All rights reserved

www.jedthecommunicator.com

This whole process has been very interesting and I truly have been blessed because of it. I have met some amazingly wonderful human beings who have only wanted to help me grow, as they will help you grow. Again, I hope that you have grown from this experience and I look forward to sharing more with you in our future projects.

Just remember one thing. These skills are NOT something you are born with. These skills are learned behaviors. If you will take action and believe that you will achieve what you have set out to achieve, you will.

I will leave you with two thoughts:

"Whatever the mind can conceive and believe, the mind can achieve."

Dr. Napoleon Hill

"When the voice and the vision on the inside become more profound and more clear and louder than the opinions on the outside, you have mastered your life."

Dr. John F. Demartini

Copyright © 2008. Jed A. Reay. All rights reserved.

www.ingramcontent.com/pod-product-compliance
Lightning Source LLC
Chambersburg PA
CBHW061632040426
42446CB00010B/1375